Asia Bible Commentary Series

RUTH

Langham
GLOBAL LIBRARY

This is a delightful commentary that deserves a wide readership. The authors combine solid exegesis with a warm and very readable style. Their exploration of the book of Ruth with Asian eyes reminds us Westerners how much closer to the world of the Bible others may be. The illustrative anecdotes from their own Indian world give this commentary a quality that is found in none other. Congratulations to the authors of the volume and the editors of the series.

Daniel I. Block, DPhil
Gunther H. Knoedler Professor Emeritus of Old Testament,
Wheaton College, Wheaton, Illinois, USA

What makes this commentary stand out from other works on the book of Ruth is the interface of the biblical text with Indian culture and stories, and with Jewish readings. The authors' engaging style draws the reader into the world of the story with its ancient background, and leads one to reflect on similar issues in contemporary Asian society. What an enjoyable book!

Athena Evelyn Gorospe, PhD
Chair, Biblical Studies Department,
Asian Theological Seminary, Manila, Philippines

Imagine yourself in the tenth century AD walking the alleys of old Damascus seeking to find the Hakawati's Café, a place where a crowd gathers every Friday evening to attentively listen to the story-teller (*hakawati*) sharing a story from the ancient past. As the audience becomes excited to reach the climax of the story the *hakawati* concludes by saying "to be continued next week."

Dr. Dharamraj is a gifted *hakawati* as she narrates the magnificent story of Ruth. She skillfully combines a solid exegesis with Asian stories and presents the reader with contemporary applications. Dr. Dharamraj will surely oblige you to read her book to its last page (no need to come back next Friday)!

I will be teaching the book of Ruth in the seminary and this book is my first choice for a reading assignment.

Riad Kassis, PhD
Director, Langham Scholars Ministry,
Langham Partnership

Visiting a famous gallery I was impressed by a certain painting. Then an art expert explained it to me, commenting on various things I had missed, such as how the artist used a breakthrough technique which displayed its brilliance. My eyes were opened and I appreciated it so much more. Reading this commentary on Ruth had a similar effect on me. It proves an excellent guide, enabling us to read Ruth through Asian eyes but also through the eyes of an expert OT scholar, committed Bible teacher, and faithful disciple of Christ. Anyone reading, teaching, or preaching Ruth cannot fail to be enriched by this volume.

Derek Tidball, PhD
Former Principal,
London School of Theology, UK

Asia Bible Commentary Series

RUTH

**Havilah Dharamraj
with
Philip Ewan Yalla**

General Editor
Federico G. Villanueva

Old Testament Consulting Editors
Yohanna Katanacho, Tim Meadowcroft, Joseph Shao

New Testament Consulting Editors
Steve Chang, Andrew Spurgeon, Brian Wintle

© 2019 by Havilah Dharamraj and Philip Ewan Yalla

Published 2019 by Langham Global Library
An imprint of Langham Publishing
www.langhampublishing.org

Langham Publishing and its imprints are a ministry of Langham Partnership

Langham Partnership
PO Box 296, Carlisle, Cumbria, CA3 9WZ, UK
www.langham.org

Published in partnership with Asia Theological Association

ATA
QCC PO Box 1454 – 1154, Manila, Philippines
www.ataasia.com

ISBNs:
978-1-78368-546-2 Print
978-1-78368-707-7 ePub
978-1-78368-709-1 PDF

British Library Cataloguing in Publication Data
A catalogue record for this book is available from the British Library.

ISBN: 978-1-78368-546-2

Cover & Book Design: projectluz.com

With much affection,
to my MDiv Class of March 2019 at SAIACS
Chrish, Deepika, Francis, Geo, Jerome, John, Muan and Selson
and to my colleague
Angu
May each explore and reach their God-given
potential to be an *ish hayil* or *esheth hayil*

CONTENTS

SERIES PREFACE

In recent years, we have witnessed one of the greatest shifts in the history of world Christianity. It used to be that the majority of Christians lived in the West, but Christians are now evenly distributed around the globe. This shift has implications for the task of interpreting the Bible from within our respective contexts, which is in line with the growing realization that every theology is contextual. Thus, the questions that we bring into our reading of the Bible will be shaped by our present realities as well as our historical and social locations. There is a need therefore to interpret the Bible for our own contexts.

The Asia Bible Commentary Series addresses this need. In line with the mission of the Asia Theological Association Publications, we have gathered evangelical Bible scholars working among Asians to write commentaries on each book of the Bible. The mission is to "produce resources that are biblical, pastoral, contextual, missional, and prophetic for pastors, Christian leaders, cross-cultural workers, and students in Asia." Although the Bible can be studied for different reasons, we believe that it is given primarily for the edification of the Body of Christ (2 Tim 3:16–17). The ABCS is designed to help pastors in their sermon preparation, cell group or lay leaders in their Bible study groups, and those training in seminaries or Bible schools.

Each commentary begins with an introduction that provides general information about the book's author and original context, summarizes the main message or theme of the book, and outlines its potential relevance to a particular Asian context. The introduction is followed by an exposition that combines exegesis and application. Here, we seek to speak to and empower Christians in Asia by using our own stories, parables, poems, and other cultural resources as we expound the Bible.

The Bible is actually Asian in that it comes from ancient West Asia, and there are many similarities between the world of the Bible and traditional Asian cultures. But there are also many differences that we need to explore in some depth. That is why the commentaries also include articles or topics in which we bring specific issues in Asian church, social, and religious contexts into dialogue with relevant issues in the Bible. We do not seek to resolve every tension that emerges but rather to allow the text to illumine the context and vice versa, acknowledging that we do not have all the answers to every mystery.

May the Holy Spirit, who inspired the writers of the Bible, bring light to the hearts and minds of all who use these materials, to the glory of God and to the building up of the churches!

Federico G. Villanueva
General Editor

LIST OF ABBREVIATIONS

BOOKS OF THE BIBLE

Old Testament

Gen, Exod, Lev, Num, Deut, Josh, Judg, Ruth, 1–2 Sam, 1–2 Kgs, 1–2 Chr, Ezra, Neh, Esth, Job, Ps/Pss, Prov, Eccl, Song, Isa, Jer, Lam, Ezek, Dan, Hos, Joel, Amos, Obad, Jonah, Mic, Nah, Hab, Zeph, Hag, Zech, Mal

New Testament

Matt, Mark, Luke, John, Acts, Rom, 1–2 Cor, Gal, Eph, Phil, Col, 1–2 Thess, 1–2 Tim, Titus, Phlm, Heb, Jas, 1–2 Pet, 1–2–3 John, Jude, Rev

BIBLE TEXTS AND VERSIONS

Divisions of the canon

NT	New Testament
OT	Old Testament

Ancient texts and versions

LXX	Septuagint
MT	Masoretic Text

Modern versions

ESV	English Standard Version
HCSB	Holman Christian Standard Bible
NASB	New American Standard Bible
NIV	New International Version
KJV	King James Version
NLT	New Living Translation

Journals, reference works, and series

BASOR	*Bulletin of the American Schools of Oriental Research*

CBQ	*Catholic Biblical Quarterly*
JBL	*Journal of Biblical Literature*
JBQ	*Jewish Bible Quarterly*
JOTT	*Journal of Translation and Textlinguistics*
JSOT	*Journal for the Study of the Old Testament*
NAC	New American Commentary
NEA	Near Eastern Archaeology
NICOT	New International Commentary on the Old Testament
NIVAC	NIV Application Commentary
OTL	Old Testament Library
VT	*Vetus Testamentum*
WBC	Word Biblical Commentary

INTRODUCTION

The theme that puts money in the banks of the Bollywood industry is boy-meets-girl. The "boy" and the "girl" are usually bursting with the sweet bloom of youthfulness; their love faces an obstacle or two, usually from the family or the community; at the end of 160 minutes, we are reassured that such stories always end with happily ever after. How many books or movies come to mind that tell the story of a not-so-young widow who meets a significantly older man?[1] That is what Ruth does.

Before we mentally shelve Ruth in the "romance" section, we must give a minute's thought to whether "romance" is all it is. Perhaps that is too narrow a categorization. The first and the last quarters of Ruth – a good half of the story! – preoccupy themselves with the condition of widowhood. These are the sections of the book in which timeless human experiences are thrown into sharp relief: inconsolable bereavement; the deep sadness of parting; the sting of tears welling out of a loss of hope; the shame of returning from a venture empty-handed; but also dreams coming true in a way that requires a pinch-me-if this-is-real; the cuddled warmth of a much longed-for baby rising into the heart; the contentment that comes from living in quiet dignity among one's own people. The central section of Ruth is indeed a version of "boy meets girl," but, the careful reader will see that the "romance" is overwhelmed by the "drama." Simply by the structure of the book, Boaz and Ruth are encircled by their families and the generations that precede and succeed them. They rest their choices – even of each other! – on the bedrock of familial loyalty. Their relationship does not take as its starting point the usual "love at first sight" but rather, the mandate of the law. The proposal of marriage is a declaration made in the town square, before an assembly of townspeople. Community blessings shower down on the marriage, like confetti at a present-day wedding. The baby born is named by the neighbors and last seen in the arms of his grandmother. The narrator coos over his cradle the names of his descendants-to-be – for in his family line lies his greatness, just as a drop of water gains its roar by dissolving into an ocean wave. Ruth transcends the "romance" genre by a mile and more. And, even though it has all the twists and turns of a roller-coaster, it moves beyond "drama." Set into families and clans, moored into a small-town population, segueing on either side into the bloodline of a tribe, and

---

1. To its credit, Bollywood has put out some wonderfully sensitive renderings of widow romance. Among them, are *Sholay* and *Prem Rog*.

setting itself into the history of a people group, this book is "history" with community at its heart.

It is for these reasons that Asians can tumble out of their everyday world straight into the world of this story. In the speeches that its characters make, in the joys and sorrows of its protagonists, in the affairs the book concerns itself with, in the values and priorities it articulates, Ruth's colors are recognizably eastern and its texture, familiarly Asian.

That is why this commentary has chosen to give more space than is usual to rabbinic readings of Ruth. The Jewish sages belonged to Asia, and the (often convoluted!) interpretations they bring to bear on the text will give us the perspective – whether we agree with it or not – of an ancient community to which this book was sacred scripture.

AUTHORSHIP AND DATE

Authorship and the date of writing are issues close to the heart of any enthusiast of history or literature. Although instructive, the answers to both these questions remain tentative at best. So far, attempts to answer the question of authorship have been the most inconclusive. This is primarily because, in keeping with the literary practices in the ancient world, the author of Ruth chose complete anonymity.[2] Down the ages, this has not deterred attempts to identify the author. For example, the Babylonian Talmud identifies Samuel as the author. On the other hand, some scholars, such as A. J. Bledstein, have proposed a female author – perhaps Tamar the daughter of king David.[3] This probability of a female author rests on the book's majoring on the concerns of women.[4] That the lady author could have been Tamar is based on the assumption that the book was "royal propaganda," seeking to legitimize, even glorify, the Moabite blood in David's veins. However attractive the options, the exercise of trying to put a name to the original author has been a futile exercise.

With regard to the date of composition, the evidence is again inconclusive. However, on grounds such as literary features within the text and the theology of the book, we may be able to make more definite assertions about date than about authorship. Over the last century, there have been strong arguments

---

2. Frederic Bush, *Ruth-Esther*, WBC 9 (Texas: Word Books, 1996), 26.
3. K. Lawson Younger, *Judges and Ruth*, NIVAC (Grand Rapids: Zondervan, 2002), 389.
4. Raymond B. Dillard and Tremper Longman III, *An Introduction to the Old Testament* (Grand Rapids: Zondervan, 2006), 131.

for a postexilic date for this book. Block lists the chief arguments presented in favor of a postexilic date for this book:

a. The Aramaic forms of Hebrew words that have been used in the book are an indication that the language has moved on from Standard Biblical Hebrew (SBH) to Late Biblical Hebrew (LBH).

b. The author provides explanatory notes to the legal custom of sandal-removal (4:7), which may suggest that the first audience of the book may be far removed in time from the period of the judges, which is the setting of the story.

c. The genealogy in chapter 4 closely parallels the "priestly" genealogies of the Pentateuch and Chronicles, which would then be evidence of a postexilic date.

d. If the favorable presentation of Ruth the Moabite was to balance out the heavily negative tone used against foreigners in Ezra and Nehemiah, the former would be dated more or less contemporaneous with the latter, which is clearly postexilic.

e. The allusion to the period of the judges could be the work of the Deuteronomist, in line with the postexilic redaction(s) of Deuteronomy.

f. In the divisions of the Hebrew canon, Ruth is placed in the third and last section, which is the Writings (*ketubim*). This section is understood to have been put together after the prophetic works (*nevi'iim*) had been canonized,[5] and so the placement gives Ruth a later rather than an earlier dating.

On the linguistic argument, some scholars hold that there is a much more extensive use of SBH than LBH, and favor a preexilic date, perhaps even as early as the time of David.[6] Bush positions the composition of Ruth between the late preexilic and early exilic period.[7] Block revisits his arguments to propose a preexilic "late seventh-century BCE date" to "accommodate both the cultural and chronological distance required between the events described and the composition of 4:7 (the original audience did not know the custom of the

---

5. Daniel I. Block, *Judges, Ruth*, NAC 6 (Nashville: Broadman & Holman, 1999), 590–591.
6. Edward F. Campbell, *Ruth: A New Translation with Introduction, Notes, and Commentary*, The Anchor Bible Commentary 7 (New York: Doubleday, 1975), 262.
7. Bush, *Ruth-Esther*, 58–59.

sandal) and account for some of the book's LBH and Aramaic features."[8] A
mediating possibility is to allow that a preexilic narrative (whether in oral or
written form) has been given a final shaping in the postexilic period.

CANONICAL STATUS AND POSITION

The canonicity of Ruth was virtually never challenged. The location of this
book, however, has varied a good deal depending on whether it was the
Septuagint or the various Hebrew Bible canons.[9] The Septuagint places Ruth
between Judges and Samuel, which is its History section (as in our English
Bibles), though in the Hebrew Bible this placement would put it in the (Early)
Prophets. The Hebrew canon consistently positions this book in the Writings
section, although in varying locations. While a significant number of scholars think Ruth originally belonged in the Writings,[10] it is nearly impossible
to determine with certainty whether Ruth started off in the Writings or in
the Prophets.[11] All we can do is to deduce the logic of the various alternative
positions in the canon Ruth has been found in.

Let us begin with the Septuagint, whose book order the Christian canon
follows, where Ruth sits between Judges and Samuel. This location is readily
understandable, since the opening verse of the book reports that the setting
of Ruth is the period of the judges. What is more, Ruth forms a contrasting
pair with Judges. First, the two differ in circumstances. The closing chapters
of Judges describe a civil war raging through the tribes, with Benjamin in
danger of being wiped off the map. Ruth, on the contrary, is a pastoral idyll,
where the people are at peace, even if they are traditional enemies as Israel
and Moab were.

Second, in Judges, covenant loyalty is in shreds. Tribes are reluctant to
honor the allegiance they owe each other in times of crisis (Judg 5:16–17),
Ephraim is quick to take offence against its brothers (Judg 8:1; 12:1), the
Jordan stains red with the blood shed by Gilead (Judg 12:4–6), Jabesh Gilead
is put to the sword (Judg 20:10–11), and Benjamin is nearly annihilated
(Judg 21:2–3). In Ruth, the actors spontaneously perform deeds of kindred
loyalty and praise each other for it. Their conversations are graced with words

---

8. Daniel I. Block, *Ruth*, Exegetical Commentary on the Old Testament: A Discourse Analysis
of the Hebrew Bible (Grand Rapids, Mich.: Zondervan, 2015), 32–33.
9. Bush, 1–2; Younger, *Judges and Ruth*, 390; Block, *Judges, Ruth*, 588.
10. Campbell, *Ruth*, 34.
11. Block, *Judges, Ruth*, 589.

of blessing, whether between a woman and her daughters-in-law, between a wealthy landlord and his employees, or between that same landlord and the destitute woman who gleans in his fields.

Third, there is adherence to the law. As Judges draws to a close, the Israelites play fast and loose with the law, repeatedly breaching it and amending it for their convenience. In complete contrast, the book of Ruth has the whole Bethlehemite community, and even a Moabite resident alien, honoring the law, not just in letter but also in spirit![12]

Fourth, there is the treatment of women. As the codes of social conduct unravel in Judges, women become the casualty. From being honored – as Achsah, Deborah, and Jael were – a woman is gang-raped, her dead body is brutalized, female prisoners of war are forcibly married off, virgins are kidnapped. In Ruth, the trajectory is in reverse. Women move from desperation to contentment, from the outer edges of community to its heart, from the stigma of an accursed lineage to matriarchy of a royal line. For all these reasons, pairing Ruth with Judges is logical.

In ancient manuscripts of the Hebrew Bible, Ruth is found in a bundle of five festal books called the *Megilloth* (scrolls). These books are sometimes arranged in a preconceived historical or chronological sequence:

> Ruth: pertaining to David
> Song of Songs: Solomon's younger years
> Ecclesiastes: Solomon's older years
> Lamentations: exilic period
> Esther: postexilic/Persian period[13]

Since the *Megilloth* sequence of books comes right after Psalms, Job, and Proverbs, the final chapter of Proverbs transitions smoothly into Ruth. The "wife of noble character" (*eshet hayil*) described in the acrostic poem in Proverbs 31:10–31 is actualized in flesh and blood in the unexpected person of a Moabite widow! Towards the end of the book, Ruth is declared an *eshet hayil* (3:11).[14]

A second arrangement found in manuscripts follows the liturgical calendar, since each scroll was read at a particular festival:[15]

---

12. Kirsten Nielsen, *Ruth: A Commentary*, OTL, trans. Edward Broadbridge (Louisville: Westminster John Knox, 1997), 20; Younger, *Judges and Ruth*, 391.
13. Younger, *Judges and Ruth*, 390.
14. Younger, 390–391.
15. See Younger, 391.

Song of Songs:	read at Passover in the month of *Nisan* (March-April)
Ruth:	read at the Feast of (seven) Weeks separating the Passover from the giving of the law at Sinai on this day; called *Shavuoth* (weeks) in Hebrew and Pentecost in Greek (for the seven weeks, rounded off to fifty days); celebrated in the month of *Sivan* (May-June)
Lamentations:	read on the ninth day of the month of *Ab* (August-September), commemorating the common day on which Jerusalem fell, in 587 BC, to Nebuchadnezzar the Babylonian, and in AD 70, to Titus the Roman.
Ecclesiastes:	read at the Feast of *Sukkoth* ("booths" or "tabernacles" or "shelters") in the month of *Tishri* (September-October)
Esther:	read for the Feast of *Purim* in the month of *Adar* (February-March), celebrating the deliverance from the hands of Haman under Persian rule.

A third arrangement in the Hebrew Bible, which comes from the Babylonian Talmud, has Ruth placed right at the beginning of the Writings, immediately following Psalms.[16] We, however, do not know the reason for this arrangement. Nevertheless, this need not bother us since the reasons for all the different placements of Ruth are, at best, deductions.

The various canonical positions of Ruth do, however, seem to influence the reading of the text. If one considers that Ruth is placed between Judges and Samuel, then a theological reading, as Lau and Goswell suggest, moves beyond the discussions of the narrative as justifying David's kingship and centers on the unfolding of the themes of "divine providence and kindness" as resting upon the Davidic dynasty and, ultimately, Israel.[17] On the other hand, the reading of Ruth after Proverbs leads to the celebration of Ruth as the embodiment of the excellent wife in Proverbs 31 who epitomizes Wisdom, as is evident in Ruth's commitment, diligence, and resourcefulness.[18] And then, the reading of Ruth as a precursor to the Psalms portrays Ruth as a devout person whose story prepares the readers for the recurring theme of many writers of psalms – God's

---

16. Younger, 391.
17. Peter H. W. Lau and Gregory Goswell, *Unceasing Kindness: A Biblical Theology of Ruth*, New Studies in Biblical Theology (Downers Grove: InterVarsity Press, 2016), 30–35.
18. Lau and Goswell, *Unceasing Kindness*, 46–50.

saving act and kindness.[19] Finally, considering Ruth as the liturgical text for the festival that commemorates the giving of the law at Sinai extols her as the model practitioner of the law – all the more ethnically subversive because she is a Moabite, and all the more culturally subversive because she is a woman.

HISTORICITY AND GENRE

While the canonicity of Ruth has hardly ever been challenged, what has been disputed is the historicity of the book – that is, were the characters in the book real people, and did the events reported in Ruth really take place? One reason for doubting the book's historicity is that in the Hebrew canon the book is not placed in the Prophets, which recounts the history of Israel, but rather in Writings, which is the more literary section. A second reason is the range of artistic elements or literary devices employed in the narrative, such as assonance and alliteration, word play, *inclusio*, and parallel paneling. This is thought to signal that Ruth was meant to be perceived only as a literary work without regard to its historical accuracy.[20] The transfer of Ruth from history into fiction does not trouble those who hold this view, since they would argue that the book's historicity is not as important as the truths it teaches. Pressler, for example, argues this position as follows:

> It should be noted that to call Ruth a story rather than history is not to say that it is somehow less than true. Great literature discloses truths unavailable through historical reports. Novels like *The Brothers Karamazov* or *The Color Purple*, for example, use the language of metaphor, fiction, and poetry to speak truths far more profound than, say, the committee minutes sitting on my desk, even though the committee minutes are more historically factual.[21]

But arguments for the historicity of the book emerge from the text itself. Block argues that, first, since the book explicitly moors the narrative within a chronological time period, we should not discount this testimony of the text. Second, the genealogy at the end of Ruth calls for treating the book as a recounting or retelling of history. Third, since Ruth does not record supernatural events,

---

19. Lau and Goswell, 69–70. Bovell starts with a chiastic structure in Ruth 1:1–6 to draw links with Proverbs on one side and Song of Songs on the other. Carlos Bovell, "Symmetry, Ruth and Canon," *JSOT* 28, no. 2 (2003): 175–191.

20. Campbell, *Ruth*, 121–124.

21. Carolyn Pressler, *Joshua, Judges and Ruth*, Westminster Bible Companion (Louisville: Westminster John Knox, 2002), 261.

it does not naturally lend itself to the necessity of being treated as a fictional work. Fourth, since this book makes a case for the legitimacy of the Davidic dynasty, Block observes that it would be counterproductive for the narrator to create a fictional story with a Moabite as David's great-grandmother. And finally, since the New Testament witnesses to the historicity of the characters in the book of Ruth (Matt 1:5), it would be unwise to discount them as fictional.[22] This said, there is a caveat: Given the artistic nature of the book, we must allow the narrator to make narrative adjustments in the story. This need not be understood as a misrepresentation of facts but rather, as artistic license.[23]

This leads us to the question of the genre of Ruth. Common options are: "folktale," "novella," "short story," and "edifying short story."[24] A folktale is a narrative with a straightforward plot, where the problem that develops moves quickly to resolution. A novella is "a fictional narrative of indeterminate length (a few pages to two or three hundred), restricted to a single event, situation, or conflict, which produces an element of suspense and leads to an unexpected turning point so that the conclusion surprises even while it is logically consistent." A short story, however, has no clear definition, given the indefiniteness of its length.[25] And, finally, as is obvious from the term, an "edifying short story" is a short story that does not merely entertain but also instructs its audiences.

Given these definitions, the historic nature of the book, the brevity of the narration, and the didactic aspects within the book, Ruth does not fit the category of a mere folktale or a novella. It is a historical short story that aims to edify its listeners.[26]

PURPOSE

The reason we spend time on issues such as the date of composition, the canonical location, and the genre of the book is to help us understand the narrator's purpose for Ruth. Considering the lack of consensus on these issues, there is difference of scholarly opinion on the purpose of the book as well.

---

22. Block, *Judges, Ruth*, 602–603; Block, *Ruth*, 36–40.
23. A good example of artistic license could be the names of the minor characters in the book, who, it would appear, are named according to their roles. (See the commentary on Elimelek and his sons in chapter 1.)
24. Younger, *Judges and Ruth*, 396.
25. Block, *Judges, Ruth*, 601.
26. This is in agreement with Block, *Judges, Ruth*, 601–603, and Younger, *Judges and Ruth*, 396–397.

One point of view is that Ruth puts forward "a Moabite heroine in a culture that often disparaged foreigners," and hence that this book "is a voice for inclusiveness."[27] Such resistance to the typical Israelite xenophobia – the fear or hatred of strangers or foreigners – is quite possible, both in the preexilic and postexilic periods. In the latter, it presents a perspective that either resists or complements that of Ezra-Nehemiah in that it welcomes into the faith community those women who embrace the faith of Israel.

Second, the book has invited comment from interpreters who read it from a woman's point of view. Some of them see Ruth as a story that lauds women making decisions and providing support to each other in difficult times. While this is mostly true, we also see that Naomi does not always view Ruth as an asset – certainly not at the start of the story. A contrary view is that the book of Ruth encourages patriarchy by presenting "Ruth as a model of self-sacrifice, giving up her homeland, her religion, her best chance for security, and even her child for the sake of the family."[28] This is certainly valid, but we shall critique the reading of the book that elevates certain culturally convenient characteristics of the lead protagonist Ruth, while skimming over or completely neglecting some others which might be a stone in the patriarchal shoe.

Third, the book's purpose could be to show God's providential salvation for Elimelek's family.[29] This is evidenced by the movements across the narrative. Between the first and the last chapters, complaint morphs into celebration,[30] emptiness is turned into fullness, and death is outdone by a genealogy of generations to come. Indeed, this book is a paragon of tight and masterful storytelling, with themes, word motifs, wordplay, and parallel structures weaving back and forth across the chapters – all to the praise of Yahweh, the character behind the scenes.

Fourth, it has been proposed that the book is political propaganda – that is, a work undertaken to legitimize the Davidic dynasty.[31] The argument is that the genealogical list that concludes the book does not merely serve the purpose of elevating this narrative in scale of importance from small-town to national. Rather, the haloes of "honor" that crown Ruth and Boaz do David credit. The upright Boaz, direct descendant of Judah, legitimizes David's right to the throne. The praiseworthy Ruth refutes any slur that might be cast on

---

27. Pressler, *Joshua, Judges and Ruth*, 262.
28. Pressler, 263.
29. Robert L. Hubbard, *The Book of Ruth*, NICOT (Grand Rapids: Eerdmans, 1988), 42.
30. Campbell, *Ruth*, 31–32.
31. Hubbard, *The Book of Ruth*, 42.

David's Moabite stock, for she is the model practitioner of the faith of Israel. Perhaps the book was composed during the reign of David, and even under his patronage, considering the need for such validation of David's ancestry.[32] This, however, is only speculation. An apologia or defense of David's pedigree could have been composed at any point in the timeline of Israelite history, right down to the postexilic period. We shall see, later, how the genealogical list that the book signs off with might be viewed as a pro-Davidic epilogue.

All these purposes have some merit. For purposes of relevance to our faith and its practice, however, we should also add that Ruth showcases the concept of *hesed*. By showing how covenant loyalty plays out in real life, it offers its readers flesh and blood examples – Ruth, Naomi and Boaz – to emulate.[33] It is this attribute of Yahweh, demonstrated in everyday practice, that earns Boaz a place in history, crowns Naomi's sunset years with contentment, and makes Ruth the mother of monarchs.

32. Dillard and Longman, *An Introduction to the Old Testament*, 131.
33. Bush, *Ruth-Esther*, 64; Younger, *Judges and Ruth*, 397.

INTRODUCTION

OUTLINE

Ruth 1
Structure
1:1–5   In the Country of Moab
1:6–18   On the Way to Bethlehem
             1:6–10   The First Exchange
             1:11–14   The Second Exchange
             1:15–18   The Third Exchange
1:19–22   Arrival in Bethlehem

Ruth 2
Structure
2:1   Opening Note
2:2   At Home
2:3–17   In the Fields
             2:3–7   Boaz Notices Ruth
             2:8–13   Boaz's First Act of Kindness
             2:14   Boaz's Second Act of Kindness
             2:15–17   Boaz's Third Act of Kindness
2:18–22   Back at Home
2:23   Closing Note
Conclusion

Ruth 3
Structure
3:1–5   At Home
3:6–15   At the Threshing Floor
3:16–18   Back at Home

Ruth 4
Structure
4:1–12   At the City Gate
4:13–17   At Boaz's Home
4:18–22   The Epilogue

Conclusion

RUTH 1

In a forest was a lake. A colony of mice lived peacefully on the edge of the water. Their peaceful days came to an end when a herd of thirsty elephants discovered the lake. Every day, the elephants would come by for a drink, their heavy feet trampling the mice underfoot. With no solution in sight, the king of the mice took his courage in his hands and presented himself before the chief of the elephants. "Oh, great one," the tiny mouse squeaked, looking up into the face of the elephant towering above him. "Please could you change your route to the lake so that our lives are spared? If you will do so, be assured that in your time of need I will remember your kindness and return the favor." The elephant chief laughed, and the sound reverberated through the trees. "Mouse," he said. "I am happy to consider your request. We shall not take this way again. But I can hardly see you coming to our help. We will not need any favors from you in return for this." The mouse and his clan thanked the elephant, and the herd did not trouble them again.

After some time, there came a night when the same herd of elephants fell into traps set by hunters. They struggled to release themselves but only got more and more entangled in the nets. In his moment of despair, the chief of the elephants remembered the promise the mice had made. He summoned an elephant that had managed to escape the traps and sent him to the mice to ask for help. The mice, on hearing of this crisis, leaped to their feet. "We should go!" they said to each other. "Here's our opportunity to return the favor the elephants did for us!"

The mice swarmed over the cords of the nets, nibbling steadily through the night. As daylight broke over the forest, the elephants were shaking themselves free from the traps. They thanked the mice, and from then on, the elephants and the mice remained friends. The wise say, "Never underestimate someone because of their appearance."[1]

In the first chapter of the book of Ruth, two protagonists emerge: Naomi and Ruth. Naomi initiates the action; Ruth follows her. Naomi makes a series of speeches; Ruth speaks only once. Naomi is the Israelite, the obvious contender for the place of lead actor; Ruth is the Moabite, and unlikely to be anything more than a supporting actress in a tale told by and for Israelites.

---

1. This fable changes across the countries where it is told. In Aesop's fable the equivalent of the elephants is a lion. In the Chinese version, the lion becomes a tiger. In all variants of the tale, the mouse remains a mouse.

But, surprisingly, through a series of reversals, we will discover that Naomi is (just!) an elephant and Ruth is the mouse.

STRUCTURE

Structurally, the opening chapter of Ruth readily divides into three sections, based on the geographical location of a certain Bethlehemite family: Ruth 1:1–5 tells of the migration to, and the sojourn in, Moab; 1:6–18 is set on the way from Moab to the hometown Bethlehem; and 1:19–22 is set in Bethlehem. The narrator invites us to travel with the family and share its experiences.

1:1–5 IN THE COUNTRY OF MOAB

The story opens with, "And it happened that . . ." This is the Hebrew equivalent of the formula that perks up a child's ears: "Once upon a time . . ." The narrator goes on to fix the story in a certain historical period: "In the days when the judges ruled" (1:1). It is a time marker that makes good sense considering the position of the book in the Christian canon. It is eased in between two heavyweights, Judges and the books of Samuel. While these longer books concern themselves with politics and governance, with explicit social and religious commentary, Ruth seems almost embarrassingly domestic. At first read, it is a family story whose plot moves from one crisis to another, all quite commonplace in India – fatal illnesses, widowhood, the rigors of a poor family living hand-to-mouth, and the difficulty of finding a match for a rather unsuitable girl. Except for one scene in the public square, its setting alternates between home and fields.

What unites Judges, Ruth, and the opening chapters of 1 Samuel is that they all are set in the same time period, the two centuries when governance lay in the hands of judges (roughly 1200–1000 BC). It is an era sandwiched between two historical events – the conquest of Canaan and the inauguration of the monarchy. Within this historical setting, the thread that ties one book to the next is the narrator's use of women characters. Judges opens with three women who act: the feisty Achsah (Judg 1:12–15); the formidable Deborah; and the resourceful Jael (Judges 4). Then comes a sorry series of women who are acted upon: Jephthah's daughter, whose life terminates in a ritual sacrifice (Judg 11:29–40); Samson's wife, who becomes the innocent casualty of a family feud (Judg 15:1–6); a Levite's concubine, whose body parts are circulated through the land (Judg 19:2–30); four hundred virgins of Jabesh Gilead who are taken prisoner of war and forcibly married off (Judg 21:10–14); and two hundred young unwed women kidnapped for marriage halfway through a festival (Judg 21:20–23). There are a couple of independent women – one commendable (Samson's mother; Judges 13) and one hardly so (his lady love Delilah; Judges 16) – but their stories are embedded into and overwhelmed by the distressing pattern of women thoroughly disempowered and victimized.

With Ruth and 1 Samuel 1–7, the narrative of the period of the judges comes to a close. Here, interestingly, there is a reversal. The women of these stories begin to resemble the ones we met at the opening of Judges. The socio-political and religious circumstances of Israel continue into further chaos. But against this bleak backdrop shines another admirable trio: Achsah, Deborah, and Jael are nicely balanced by the persevering Naomi, the determined Ruth, and the woman who overcame odds to give Israel its last and greatest judge, Hannah (1 Sam 1). When seen in this larger arrangement of stories that prominently feature women, it makes sense that the narrator should open the book with a marker that clearly locates Naomi and Ruth within this time period. Here is a story – he seems to be saying – that happens in the "dark ages" of Israel's history.

As if to confirm the challenges of living in such days, the opening sentence concludes with a description of adversity: a famine is raging through the land. To the narrator's original audience, this makes for an ominous start. Deuteronomy establishes that rain is a reward God reserves for his people when they behave themselves: "The LORD will open the heavens, the storehouse of his bounty, to send rain on your land in season" (Deut 28:12). Understood within the context of Israel's covenant relationship with God, the experience of blessings, which was seen as being favored by God, hinged upon their obedience to him, while their disobedience was seen as a compromise in this relationship, eventually inviting curses on them.[2] Thus, if they "do not obey the LORD" and "do not carefully follow all his commands" (Deut 28:15), then they invite curses upon themselves, among which is famine: "the LORD will strike you with . . . scorching heat and drought, with blight and mildew . . . the sky over your head will be bronze, the ground beneath you iron. The LORD will turn the rain of your country into dust and powder; it will come down from the skies until you are destroyed" (Deut 28:22–24; compare Amos 8:11–12). In an arid country like Canaan, whose perennial source was limited to the

---

2. James McKeown, "Blessings and Curses," in *Dictionary of the Old Testament: Pentateuch*, eds. T. Desmond Alexander and David W. Baker (Downers Grove, IL: InterVarsity Press; Leicester: Inter-Varsity Press, 2003), 841–885.

snow-fed Jordan, rains in the spring and autumn were critical to the economies of livestock keeping and farming.

This understanding of God as the rain-giver plays out in a later story, where the prophet Elijah pronounces a curse of drought brought on by the crown's idolatrous practices (1 Kgs 16:29–17:1). Similarly, in India, it is not unusual – especially in the rural areas with an agriculture-based economy – for people to understand a drought and the ensuing famine in religious terms. The gods are withholding rains because they are angry. Of course, why they are angry is irrelevant, and perhaps even an irreligious question to ask. What is of pressing urgency is that they need to be appeased with the right rituals. This traditional understanding of the deity is common to a great many belief systems in the world, especially ones that have an agro-economy. The God of the Old Testament, however, differs in that his actions are not arbitrary but a direct response to the disloyalty of his people. If he punishes them by withholding the seasonal rains, it is to alert them to the dangers of the path they have chosen. In Ahab's case, this king is so beguiled by the deities of the more powerful neighboring nations that he neglects God-given law. This has immediate consequences on society. Justice is replaced with corruption and its attendant evils (1 Kgs 21).

On the other hand, we should also understand that not *all* droughts were punitive. For example, there are the famines that drove several generations of the ancestors of Israel to migrate: Abraham moves to Egypt (Gen 12:10), Isaac to Gerar (Gen 26:1), and Jacob and his family to Egypt (Gen 43). The pattern of "sojourning" – living awhile in another place – is common to all these stories. In several of these cases, the Lord either initiates or endorses the migration, as in the case of Isaac's move to Philistia (Gen 26:1–3) or Jacob's to Egypt (Gen 46:1–4). Similarly, the Shunammite woman moved to Philistia on receiving Elisha's advice to "Go away with your family and stay for a while wherever you can, because the LORD has decreed a famine in the land that will last seven years" (2 Kgs 8:1). She promptly returned at the end of this period. It appears then, that temporary relocation to a neighboring country was fairly usual in times of prolonged food scarcity.

Reading Ruth in continuity with Judges that precedes it and 1 Samuel 1–7 that follows it makes it clear that Israel is doing everything it should to deserve a good famine, one so vigorous that hope fails and people emigrate. Indeed, traditional Jewish exegesis has God speaking to himself thus: "At that time said the Holy One, blessed be He, 'My children are [in] rebellion. But as to exterminating them, that is not possible, and to bring them back to Egypt is not possible, and to trade them for some other nation is something I cannot do. But this shall I do for them: lo, I shall . . . afflict them with famine in the days when the judges judge.'"[3] Given this, and given that there is no indication that Elimelek makes his move under divine direction, we readers wonder if this sojourn – however short or long – will lead the family to a happy situation.

So a man from Bethlehem in Judah moves to Moab, taking with him his wife and two sons. Twice the narrator draws the reader's attention to the detail that this man's family has moved from Bethlehem (1:1, 2) – the town whose name translates "house/granary of bread," probably owing to the region's produce of wheat and barley, almonds and grapes. Ironically, the "house of bread" lies empty. A second reason the narrator emphasizes Bethlehem, specifying that it is "Bethlehem in Judah," could be to distinguish it from Bethlehem in Zebulun, far away up the length of the land in northern Galilee (Josh 19:15–16). This location marker would have signaled to Israelite readers that the story was set in the birthplace of the great king David himself, and thus gripped them from the start. What is more, Elimelek is an Ephrathite. This, too, anticipates David, whose father Jesse was similarly a native of Ephrathah (1 Sam 17:12) – which was either an alternate name for Bethlehem or the district in which Bethlehem was located (4:11).[4]

The ancient reader would also have passed an unfavorable verdict on Elimelek's destination. This is the nation that was birthed by incest between Lot and his daughter (Gen 19:30–38) – a people of despicable origin. Historically, Moab never was friends with Israel, even though related by the kinship between Abraham and Lot. As Israel traveled from Egypt to Canaan, and came to Moab's borders, Moab took fright and resorted to hiring a prophet to curse Israel (Numbers 22–24). Moab failed to consider that Israel had demonstrated exemplary behavior so far, always opening negotiations with a polite request for peaceful passage through the lands bordering Canaan (Num 20:14–17; 21:21–22). In fact, Israel was under strict instructions from the Lord not to ignite hostilities with its future neighbors, Moab included (Deut 2:9). Moab's tactics to disempower Israel ran the range familiar to us in international diplomacy. While, on one hand, it was rattling sabers, on the other, it seduced

---

3. Jacob Neusner, *Ruth Rabbah: An Analytical Translation* (Atlanta: Scholars Press, 1989), 31.
4. Eugene H. Merrill locates the Ruth story in the Bethlehem trilogy that starts in the closing chapter of the previous book of Judges. In the first two stories, the Bethlehemites bring dishonor to their town. One presides over an idolatrous shrine (Judg 17–18) while the other incites a civil war that nearly wipes out a tribe (Judg 19–21). Elimelek's family, however, will bring it lasting fame through its connection with David. "The Book of Ruth: Narration and Shared Themes," *BSac* 142.566 (1985): 130–141, here, 131–133.

Israel into a honey trap (Num 25:1–3). In a story that features a Moabite woman as the main protagonist, it is relevant to recall that the price Israel paid for its brief frolic with Moabite women and their gods was a heavy one – a bloody purge (Num 25:1–5, 9). For their hostile intent, Moab was not to be welcomed into Israelite community even down to the tenth generation (Deut 23:3–6). In times as recent as the early judges, Moab had again shown itself less than friendly by crossing over the Jordan and occupying Israelite lands for nearly two decades (Judg 3:15–30). At this point in the story, however, while Israel's house of bread remained empty, the fields of Israel's enemy prospered! So, even though Moab stood historically condemned for refusing bread and water to Israel as it traveled up from Egypt to Canaan (Deut 23:4–5), here is an Israelite who goes to the same country to "beg for bread."[5]

Thus an Israelite family finds itself sojourning in Moab.[6] A sojourner's social position hung precariously between that of native and foreigner. Often, the sojourner would be at the mercy of the local inhabitants, with legal rights granted or withdrawn at will.[7] Added to this, ethnic conflicts were almost certain to add challenges to the sojourner's life, not unlike the tensions we see today with the migration of people groups reaching phenomenal proportions. The sojourn in Moab promises subsistence, but would the experience of living "on the wrong side of the Jordan"[8] prove to be a happy one?

With dizzying speed, the narrator introduces us to the six characters in the family, and covers the events of about a decade in just five verses. These events precipitate a crisis which the rest of the book will solve.

The narrator introduces his reader to the members of the sojourning family: a wife and two sons. The sons must have been born sickly to receive the names they do: Mahlon (possibly meaning "to be sick") and Kilion (possibly meaning "to be consumed"). These names occur nowhere else in the OT, so, one wonders if the narrator has given them whimsical names suited to their role in the story, indicating that they will take ill and die young.[9] Judaism sees in Kilion's name the anticipation that his line will disappear forever.[10] If Mahlon lives on, it will only be because of Ruth.

---

5. Moshe Alshich, *The Book of Ruth: A Harvest of Majesty*, trans. Ravi Shahar, based on an original draft by Leonard Oschry (Jerusalem: Feldheim Publishers, 1992), 541–555.
6. The word translated "to live" in verse 1 literally means "sojourn."
7. Bush, *Ruth-Esther*, 63.
8. Ellen F. Davis and Margaret Adams Parker, *Who Are You, My Daughter? Reading Ruth through Image and Text* (Louisville: Westminster John Knox, 2003), 6.
9. Block, *Judges, Ruth*, 625.
10. Alshich, *A Harvest of Majesty*, 63.

The name of the husband is Elimelek, meaning "My God is King." This is ironic for a man who removes himself from the jurisdiction of that king and moves into a land that has other gods. Elimelek plays no further part than to die and leave his family widowed and fatherless. His departure makes room for the Lord to act, and, eventually, to demonstrate that he is indeed the caring "king" who provides for his subjects[11] – whether it be the breadless townsfolk in Bethlehem, the widowed and child-bereft Naomi, or the Moabite woman Ruth who opts into this unfortunate family. The name of the wife, Naomi, means "good, pleasant, lovely."[12] As the story progresses, we shall see that her life in Moab is nothing like her name.[13]

The story of Elimelek is a story told many times over in rural India. There was a time when every year, without fail, the south-west monsoons arrived on a set date in a given region, bearing their precious gift of water. It is not so anymore. The rains in India have been as fickle as the weather worldwide. "Farmer suicides" are now simply yet another peculiar socioeconomic phenomenon. Those who give up on the rains move to the cities. There is even a term for them – "climate change refugees." Theirs are migrations fueled by hope.

We know that not all refugees realize their hopes. "Mountains look smooth from a distance," cautions popular wisdom. So it is with Elimelek and his family. From Bethlehem, their journey could have taken them down into the Rift Valley, across the Jordan, and then up the valley again, before they turned south towards the mountain ranges of Moab. Or they may have traveled south along the Dead Sea and crossed the Rift Valley at a point opposite to Moab, leaving them again with mountains to negotiate before arriving at their destination. It was an arduous passage. The hope of the refugees to find happier living conditions perhaps comes through better in the Hebrew:

A man *went* from the *House of Bread* in Judah to live awhile in *the fields of Moab*

> He and his wife, and his two sons
> And the name of the man was Elimelek
> And the name of his wife, Naomi
> And the names of his two sons, Mahlon and Kilion –

---

11. See, Davis and Parker, *Who Are You, My Daughter?*, 5.
12. Bush, *Ruth-Esther*, 64.
13. For a piquant exploration of names in the book of Ruth, see Raphael B. Schuchat, "The Use of Symbolism and Hidden Messages in the Book of Ruth," *JBQ* 30, no. 2 (2002): 110–117.

> Ephrathites from the *House of Bread* in Judah; and they *arrived* in *the fields of Moab* and lived there (1:1–2).

Notice how the opening and closing lines link and repeat phrases: the family "went" from and "arrived" in; they went from a paradoxically breadless Bethlehem to fields they hoped would sustain them. The family, we are told, settles into life in Moab: they "lived there."[14]

How quickly the narrator completes the narrative of the family's dashed hopes! In the space of two verses (1:3–4), the head of the house dies, the sons marry, a decade passes, and the two sons die also. The mountains of Moab were rocky after all, and its fields could feed them but not keep them alive. We are not told what the men died of – the narrator is impatient to get on to where his story really starts.

With Elimelek's passing, Naomi is "left with her two sons" to take care of. Whereas, in the previous verses, Naomi was referred to as "his [Elimelek's] wife," and Mahlon and Kilion were addressed as "his [Elimelek's] . . . two sons," now the point of reference shifts to Naomi. Elimelek is referred to as "Naomi's husband" and the sons as "her two sons." While the family tried to escape death by emigration, death appears to have followed them to Moab.

With the marriages of the sons, two new members are added into the family. The daughters-in-law – Orpah (meaning "neck") and Ruth (meaning "companion") – are Moabite women.[15] But here is a family without a head. Perhaps this is why the sons marry as they do, in violation of Israelite law. Deuteronomy 7:3–4 lists the nations that Israel must not marry into for fear of being led into idolatry. Although Moab is missing in the list, the principle applies, since Moabites worshiped Chemosh as their national deity (1 Kgs 11:33).[16] Centuries later, Nehemiah would violently object to Israelite men whose children could not even speak Hebrew because their mothers were "from Ashdod, Ammon and Moab" (Neh 13:1–3, 23–27). Therefore, the marriages

---

14. Here, the Hebrew word for "lived" is different from the one in verse 1. The word in verse 2 has a sense of "remaining or staying on" for an indefinite duration. Hubbard, *The Book of Ruth*, 91.

15. Orpah could derive from the noun עֹרֶף ("back of the neck") and the related verb "to turn one's back." Ruth is probably from the noun רְעוּת ("friendship") which derives from the noun רֵעַ ("friend" or "companion"). Orpah will turn her back on Naomi, while Ruth will cling to her in lifelong companionship. Thus, these names might depict character rather than actual names. This may be the case for the other names in the book as well.

16. Block, *Judges, Ruth*, 629. Judaism defends the inclusion of Ruth into the Israelite community of faith by tendentious means: The Law prohibits marriage to Moabite *men* and thus, does not apply to Israelites/Jews marrying Moabite women. *Talmud Yebamoth* 69a.

of Naomi's sons set up the possibility that this Israelite family would soon be assimilated into Moabite ways.[17] Going by the story of Lot and his gradual absorption into Sodom, the reader anticipates that nothing good will come of these marriages.

The migration that was intended "for a while" (1:1) lengthens to a decade. If there had been hope that the passing of Elimelek would be compensated by grandchildren, that hope seems to have proved empty by the end of the verse (1:4).[18] The unresolvable question is: Exactly how long did the family live in Moab?[19] If it was ten years in all before Naomi decided to return, then Ruth would have been a young widow. This makes her decision to follow Naomi to Bethlehem surprising, for she could have set the mistake of a foreign marriage behind her and started all over again. If it was ten years after the marriages of the sons, then Ruth would have been childless for a decade. This is in startling contrast to the fertile "fields of Moab" mentioned five times in this chapter (Heb 1:1–2, 6 [twice], 22).[20] Ruth remains barren, while the countryside around her yields. Indeed, even Bethlehem will celebrate a barley harvest before the chapter ends. But barren women who birth children of significance is a recurring OT theme. When Ruth does conceive, her pregnancy is all the more a matter of divine favor (4:13), and places her in the league of the matriarchs – Sarah, Rebekah, and Rachel, all of whom conceived after long periods of barrenness (Gen 11:30; 16:1; 25:21; 29:31) – and in the company of Manoah's wife, who bore a miracle child under similar circumstances (Judg 13).

An Indian saying reflects the thinking in many eastern communities: "A house without children is a graveyard." But not only are the Moabite wives barren; worse, their husbands die. Traditionally, Indians would understand this as the ill-luck brought in by the daughters-in-law, especially if it quickly followed the marriage. Ill-omened daughters-in-law are usually those born under the sign of the planet *Mangal* (Mars), who bring with them the *manglik dosha* (the inauspicious taint of Mars). Among other things, they are unlikely to birth male children, they bring misfortune into the family, they may be prone to immoral behavior, and they may bring about the death of their husband. A similar superstition existed among the ancient West Asian peoples (see Judah

---

17. Nielsen, *Ruth*, 44.
18. Hubbard, *The Book of Ruth*, 95.
19. See Davis and Parker, *Who Are You, My Daughter?*, 10–11.
20. See André LaCocque, *Ruth: A Continental Commentary*, trans. K. C. Hanson (Minneapolis: Augsburg Fortress, 2004), 38.

and Tamar). Whether Naomi viewed Orpah and Ruth as jinxed women we cannot say, but there is another point here that the plotline is trying to make.

The Canaanite pantheon included *Ra'av* ("Famine") and *Mot* ("Death") as deities. This was in much the same way that Indian religious traditions personify diseases, and attempt to appease them before they unleash their disfavor. In Telugu, the common childhood illness of chicken pox is the goddess *Aatalamma* ("the Playful Lady"), while the more fatal small pox is *Pedda Ammavaaru* ("The Senior Lady"). How ironic that the Ephrathite family fled from "Famine" only to fall into the bony hands of "Death" – from the frying pan into the fire. Here the Hebrew narrator intensifies the pathos of Naomi's loss by referring to the deceased not with a usual Hebrew word for sons (*ben*) but with a word usually used for "children" or "boys" (*yeled*).[21] (When we reach the end of the book, we shall see that this word is part of the narrator's reversal schema. For the two "children" that Naomi loses here, she will gain two others – a baby grandson and Ruth herself – who the neighbors will deem better than "seven sons" [4:14–16].) What is more, as in Indian traditions, to die and be buried in a foreign land was undesirable. In fact, it was considered the ultimate punishment from God (Amos 7:17).[22]

> And Elimelek, Naomi's husband, died and she *was left*, she and her two sons.
> They took Moabite wives; the name of one was Orpah and the name of the other, Ruth.
> And they lived there some ten years,
> Then both Mahlon and Kilion also died,
> And Naomi [alone] *was left* without her two [children] and her husband. (1:3–5)

The poignancy of Naomi's situation at either end of the decade takes on depth in the Hebrew with the use of the verb *sha'ar* ("to remain/be left over"). Used sometimes for the one bereaved,[23] it is more often used to describe those who have survived a disaster – for example, the ones that made it through the flood (Gen 7:23), those whom Joseph saved from the great famine (Gen 45:7), and those who returned from the Babylonian exile.[24] It is in this deeper sense that

---

21. Nielsen, *Ruth*, 44.
22. Block, *Judges, Ruth*, 628.
23. For example, Gen 7:23; 14:10; 42:38; Exod 14:28; Hubbard, *The Book of Ruth*, 92.
24. In Isaiah 7:3, Shear-Jashub is the name of Isaiah's son, which means "a remnant shall return." Compare Isa 10:21–22, in which Ahaz is given a reminder of impending judgment to Israel but

Elimelek and his sons are – to use a common English phrase – "survived by Naomi." Naomi, who outlived her husband – a situation bad enough in a patriarchal culture – now outlives both her children, a domestic tragedy in any culture. Rather than come through these mishaps as the lucky survivor, each bereavement leaves her increasingly lonely and vulnerable, even more so because she is a foreigner where she lives. With neither husband nor sons to care for her, a widow's options in the ancient world would have been to sell herself into slavery, to eke out a living through prostitution, or to die of neglect. Very quickly, the story seems to have come to an end – or at least, a reversal of hope to despair. Like Job, Naomi's story has begun with a sequence of bereavements that wipe out all her immediate blood relatives. The family now consists of a clutch of three widows. A traditional Hindu could not conceive of anything more ill-fated and inauspicious! In some Indian languages, a swear word to use against a single or married woman is the colloquial word for widow, as in the Kannada *munde*.

1:6–18 ON THE WAY TO BETHLEHEM

The style of this section (1:6–18) contrasts with that of 1:1–5. The breakneck pace now slows down. The narrator fleshes out the characters through dialogue, which will continue to be the primary narrative technique in the rest of the book.[25] With the narrator barely providing any additional insight into the thoughts and the feelings of the characters by way of narrative comments, the reader must listen carefully and watch the characters closely in order to understand them. Thus, for example, we note the high frequency of the verb "return/go back" (once each in 1:6, 7, 8, 10, 11, 12, 16; twice in 1:15). This key word invites the reader to notice who is returning and where to.

In this section, Naomi comes to life as the verbs concerning her take a lively turn.[26] At the end of the previous section, she "was left" (1:5). But now she acts: she hears, she prepares to return, she leaves her home, she sets out on the road to Bethlehem, and will give some rather long speeches.

One feature of this section common to the previous one is the fact that the shape of the family changes, albeit more subtly, and following the contours of the dialogue. In the first dialogue, we find "Naomi on the one side and Orpah

---

with hope of restoration. In Zechariah 8, it becomes a prophetical term for the return. Havilah Dharamraj, *A Prophet Like Moses?* (Milton Keynes: Paternoster, 2011), 125–130.
25. Bush, *Ruth-Esther*, 71.
26. See Davis and Parker, *Who Are You, My Daughter?*, 13.

and Ruth in concert on the other; in the second . . . the alliance of Orpah and Ruth is ended; in the third . . . a new alliance is created between Naomi and Ruth, and Orpah is marginalized."[27] Diagrammatically, the shifts are:

Exchange 1 (1:6–10): Naomi + (Ruth and Orpah)
Exchange 2 (1:11–14): Naomi + Ruth + Orpah
Exchange 3 (1:15–18): (Naomi + Ruth) + Orpah[28]

1:6–10 The First Exchange

With the deaths of all the males in the household, the storyline has funneled into a dead end. But here is where the narrator whips out his favorite story-telling technique: the reversal. Notice the word order in the Hebrew: "Then she arose, she and her daughters-in-law, and she returned from the fields of Moab for she had heard in the fields of Moab that the Lord had visited his people to give to them bread" (1:6; translation mine). The Hebrew signs off the verse with a flourish of alliterating words, the last one smuggling in an association with Naomi's hometown Bethlehem: *latet lahem lakhem* (*lekhem*), "to give to them bread." The narrator builds up the suspense in the sentence and then tops it off with his surprise – there is bread again!

This is the first of the few mentions of God in this book, and it is an encouraging one – God reverses, God restores! We notice also that this verse signals the closure of the Moab episode. It twice repeats "fields of Moab," balancing with a similar repetition of the phrase in 1:1–2. Here is a contrast between the fields of Moab and the land of Israel, as in the beginning of the previous section. In the previous section, one of the most essential elements of sustenance – food – was missing from the land of Israel, whereas the fields of Moab had so much of it that it could support even the immigrant families from the drought-stricken land of Israel. Here, on the contrary, as Nielsen observes, following Moab's failure to sustain the lives of the immigrants, Naomi's family is on its way back to Israel, since the Lord has restored in Israel the essential conditions that sustain life.[29] Moab is now in the past, and our faces are set towards Bethlehem.

Naomi's return is ignited by the news that the Lord has visited "his peo-ple" (1:6). Clearly, she considers herself one belonging to that community and desires to go home. But what about the Moabites Orpah and Ruth?

---

27. From Block, *Judges, Ruth*, 630, with minor changes.
28. Block, 630.
29. Nielsen, *Ruth*, 45.

Accompanying a parting guest on the first lap of the journey seems to have been customary in ancient times (see Gen 18:22–23).[30] Was this such a gesture from Ruth and Orpah? Perhaps not, since shortly thereafter Naomi attempts to persuade them to return. Once a woman marries, her identity dissolves into that of the new family. This was so in ancient West Asia as much as in many of our Asian cultures today. Thus, when Tamar's husbands die, the father-in-law was responsible to make alternative provision for her care (Gen 38:6–10). When he does not, and resorts to sending her away to her maternal home, she is entitled to fault him. Naomi's situation is similar. The Moabite girls are under her guardianship. This is familiar to Indians. Even after the husband's death, some ancient oriental law codes such as *Manusmriti* demand of a "virtuous wife" (*Manu* 5.160), loyalty to the house into which a woman marries. Sometimes, the in-laws may require the bride to change her name to one of their choice, giving her a whole new identity post-marriage. Even in widowhood, the woman continues to be the in-laws' responsibility. In Naomi's case, the blessing that she pronounces on the young widows (1:8–9) urges the young Moabite widows to return to their parental home and find another man to marry.

So the three set out. That Orpah and Ruth pack up and accompany Naomi follows the pattern at the start of the book. Just as Elimelek moves, and his family with him, now Naomi moves and her family – what is left of it – go with her. The verb "to set out" (*yatza*; 1:7) trembles with canonical freight. *Yatza* is used extensively (in its *hiphil* stem) to describe Israel setting out from Egypt, whether in the narrative in the book of Exodus or in the many recollections of the event in the rest of the OT. It is the verb that describes the release of the indentured servant in his seventh year of servitude (Exod 21:2). In the forty-ninth year, the Year of Jubilee, property is said to *yatza* (revert) to its original owner (Lev 25:28). Judah's return from the Babylonian exile is repeatedly described with *yatza* (see Ezek 20:41). To a postexilic audience of Ruth, Naomi's *yatza* is read against these other, greater, instances of "setting out." It is a verb that turns away from distress and looks forward in hope.

On the road to Bethlehem, however, Naomi begins to reconsider. She makes a suggestion to her daughters-in-law, worded as an instruction not to go with her (1:8–9a). Naomi begins by blessing the Moabites in the name of the Lord. (We should be aware that the fully capitalized "LORD" in English translations is, in the Hebrew, Yahweh – the personal name of Israel's God.)

---

30. Pressler, *Joshua, Judges and Ruth*, 269.

Does the Yahwistic blessing mean that all three women are Yahweh-worshipers? This need not be the case at all. In fact, Naomi will later recommend that Ruth, like Orpah, should return to "her gods" (1:15). In a religiously pluralistic context, such as in many parts of Asia, we may find this language familiar. A Christian can bless a Hindu in the name of Christ – think of the graduation prayers said over a multi-faith student body in a Protestant school. Naomi need not necessarily believe that the authority of the Lord extends into the territory of Moab; she may have assumed that he was like the deities of other nations, whose jurisdiction is limited to the lands that worship them.[31] Rather, Orpah and Ruth have been good daughters-in-law, who have "shown kindness" (*hesed*) to her, and this is Naomi's way of acknowledging it. Although the English may sound somewhat watery, we shall see in the next chapter that *hesed* is a weighty Hebrew word, thick with meaning.

Why does Naomi want her daughters-in-law to return to Moab?[32] She is not shirking her responsibilities. Rather, she is working out how best they may be fulfilled. Clearly, her responsibility is to see the widows married again. Marriage is so much a woman's insurance against all manner of evils that, in a similar cultural context in India, we bless a bride with the words *Sada sumangali raho* ("stay a married woman forever"). Among names for girl babies is *Sumangala* ("well married").

Is there any significance in Naomi asking her daughters-in-law to return to their "mother's home" rather than to their father's house?[33] Perhaps she sees the girls moving from one mother (herself) to another (their own). In the Indian context, the "mother's house" is the place a married woman traditionally

---

31. Block, *Judges, Ruth*, 633.
32. For a sociological investigation of the working of the minds of these three widows as they engage with each other and come to their individual decisions (and for the shifts in Ruth's identity within the Bethlehemite community) see Victor H. Matthews, "The Determination of Social Identity in the Story of Ruth," *Biblical Theology Bulletin* 36, no. 2 (2006): 16–27. https://doi.org/10.1177/01461079060360020101.
33. Western commentators find here a puzzle to solve: While various commentators explain the reason for this phrase variously, Block and Hubbard seem to offer a lexically sound explanation, while Bush's observation from the immediate context of the narrative seems to offer yet another sensible explanation to the phrase "mother's house." Block and Hubbard observe that this phrase ("mother's house") occurs only in three other places in the OT, namely in Song of Songs 3:4; 8:2, and Genesis 24:28. While in Song of Songs, the lady refers to the "mother's house" as a secure place to be intimate with her lover, in Genesis, Rebecca goes to her "mother's house" to report her conversation with Eliezer regarding the marriage proposal brought by Eliezer on behalf of his master Abraham's son, Isaac. Hence, both in Song of Songs and in Genesis, "mother's house" has strong associations with love and marriage. Hence they assume that the entreaty to return to the "mother's house" in Ruth is an entreaty to find love and enter marriage. Block, *Judges, Ruth*, 632; Hubbard, *The Book of Ruth*, 86.

returns to when close to delivering a baby; the place she flees to should her new family harass her for dowry; the place she seeks out for rest and refreshment when the children have school holidays; the place of refuge should she become divorced or widowed. In contrast, the term "father's house" is more frequently used when speaking of legal rights to property – and thus largely within the male domain – or if a woman is staking a claim to inheritance. Perhaps this is the sense in which Naomi urges the girls to return to their "mother's home," since they will find there the future that they would not as foreigners in Israel – their Moabite "mother's home" is likely to provide passage to "the home of another husband" (1:8).

Even before the young women could respond to her command, Naomi makes a gesture of parting by kissing them (1:9b–10). Her speech and goodbye kiss obviously stir up the emotions of all three women, leading them to weep bitterly.[34] As is common in some eastern cultures, such as India, there is an uninhibited show of feeling.[35] But the daughters-in-law also demonstrate the fidelity we would expect of any traditionally minded woman. While Naomi's people are not their own, they recognize that they are under a social – and perhaps even an emotional – obligation. On the other hand, it is possible that the conversation, in typical oriental fashion, has not yet reached its completion. A generous offer is made. The other party courteously declines. The offer is made again in terms that leave no doubt that the offer is genuine. The other party usually accepts.

The young women speak for the first time in verse 10. They use the opening verb from Naomi's speech ("Go back/return") and turn it around: "We will go back [return]," they say, "[not to our mother's home, but] with you to your people." These words cannot, however, be dismissed as a customary polite gesture, since these young women have, in the past, genuinely demonstrated

---

34. The phrase "they wept aloud" is literally "they raised their voices and wept." Bush observes that the word "their voices" in this verse takes a plural ending and not a dual ending. Therefore, the narrator seems to be implying that all three women wept, not just the two daughters-in-law.
35. My doctoral student Angukali Rotokha pointed out that we should concede that in a few Indian subcultures such a show of emotion is discouraged. In Rajasthan, for instance, family members of the upper caste, women in particular, are prohibited from publicly expressing their grief over the deceased. Even in such cases, however, emotions are expressed, even if vicariously, through professional mourners called *rudaalis* – lower-caste women who earn a living by expressing grief on behalf of the family. Underlying the profession of the *rudaalis* is the twofold idea that the upper-caste women should not lose their dignity before commoners, and that the tears and emotions of the *rudaalis* are tradable commodities available for the rich upper caste to buy. These in turn point to the deeper issues of caste, gender, and economic disparity in the society.

hesed ("shown kindness") to Naomi. Nevertheless, the level of commitment embedded in their words has to be examined in the exchange that follows.

In the postexilic period, the reader would immediately pick up the motif-word *shub* ("return"). To a community that has only just returned from the Babylonian captivity, the word quivers in resonance with the prophets who had promised a "return." There is a basic sense of returning to a homeland that they had recalled with tears: "By the rivers of Babylon we sat and wept when we remembered Zion" (Ps 137:1; see Isa 35:10; 51:11; Jer 31:8). Beyond this, there is the theological sense. *Shub* is, arguably, the prophet's vocabulary for repentance, for turning back to the God Judah had covenanted to love (Isa 31:6; 44:22; Jer 3:1–4:1; 24:7; Ezek 16:55; Hos 6:1; Joel 2:12; Zech 1:3; Mal 3:7). Against this prophetic theme, the voices of the two Moabite women harmonize with the desire of the exiled to seek a future in Israel and in Israel's God.

1:11–14 The Second Exchange

Naomi will not give in so easily to the rhetoric of her daughters-in-law. And so she entreats them with the vocative "my daughters." Here is a form of address familiar to Indian ears. Girl children and younger women are *beti* ("daughter") not just to their parents but also to their in-laws and communities. That Naomi uses "daughter" rather than "daughter-in-law" would not surprise an Indian. In-laws would use the two synonymously, though we could concede that Naomi's voice has now taken on a tone of tender pleading. Perhaps she hopes that the tender vocative ("my daughters") would avail more than her previous imperative ("Go back").

Naomi speaks again – forcefully and at length. In fact, this is the longest speech in the book! Over and over she uses rhetorical questions to make her point, as we often do. "If I asked you to, would you jump into a well?" we may ask; and that question concludes our case. It is an effective tool to use in argumentation because it leaves the addressee with only one answer, the one the speaker wishes to elicit.

On a first reading, Naomi's speech sounds like the ramblings of an agitated elderly woman. But, on closer observation, a structure emerges. Naomi opens with her instruction for return, quickly following it up with a rhetorical question. The question suggests that there is no good reason for the Moabites to go with her. The answer to this primary rhetorical question will come at the very end of her argument (1:11–13).

Instruction: But Naomi said, "Return home, my daughters"; (v. 11; also v. 8)

Primary question: Why would you come with me? (v. 11)

Argument 1: I have no sons to wed you

Secondary question raised	Am I going to have any more sons, who could become your husbands? (v. 11)
Secondary question answered	Return home, my daughters; I am too old to have another husband. (v. 12)

Argument 2: Even if I should bear sons now, you could not wed them

Hypothesis raised	Even if I thought there was still hope for me – even if I had a husband tonight and then gave birth to sons, (v. 12)
Hypothesis countered	would you wait until they grew up? Would you remain unmarried for them? No, [of course not][36] my daughters (v. 13)

Answer to the primary question	It is more bitter for me than for you, because the LORD's hand has turned against me! (v. 13)

Thus Naomi's instruction validated

The premise driving the argument that Orpah and Ruth will gain nothing by going with Naomi is this: Naomi will *not* provide another son as husband for each widowed daughter-in-law. This premise is in line with the system of levirate marriage practiced among the ancient West Asian peoples – it is both an ancient custom (Gen 38) and coded in the Mosaic law (Deut 25:5–10). According to this system, if a married man dies leaving his widow childless, the brother of the dead man (the widow's brother-in-law) would marry the widow, and the child born to them from that marriage would raise a name for the dead man (compare Matt 22:23–33). We will deal with this in greater

---

36. See NLT: "No, of course not, my daughters!"

detail in chapter 3. Perhaps the daughters-in-law are placing their hope in a levirate marriage once they reach Israel.[37]

Even if Naomi had levirate marriage in mind, her concern seems to be obtaining security for the young widows rather than raising a name for her dead sons. Moreover, whatever purpose of the levirate system she had in mind, Naomi's argument here is about the impossibility of the levirate hope. Using such absurd hypothetical cases to persuade or dissuade people is common even in the Indian subcontinent. But the reader who knows the rest of the story smiles at this point because, as it turns out, Naomi will miss no opportunity to "catch" a husband for Ruth. Even if not from her own womb, she will excitedly identify Boaz as a possible *levir* and hatch a devious (and dubious!) scheme to get him to marry Ruth. Using two arguments – one a realistic rhetorical question concerning her biological age and widowed state, and the other a fanciful hypothesis on a future marriage and sons, an *argumentum ad absurdum* – Naomi dismisses any possibility that she can provide a secure home for Orpah and Ruth.

These questions seem to have elements of care, frustration, and helplessness embedded in them. While, on the one hand, these questions show that Naomi is seriously concerned about the young women finding "rest [security] in the home of another husband" (1:9), she also seems frustrated by the fact that she would not be able to provide those husbands to them. The literal translation of the second question would be close to the ESV rendering: "Have I yet sons in my womb that they may become your husbands?" (1:11). The word used for "womb" is different from the usual Hebrew word for a woman's womb. Commentators note that the word used here is used elsewhere in the Hebrew Bible for the visceral organs (intestines) of both men and women,[38] the seat of a person's emotions (compare Isa 16:11). Naomi's feelings of helplessness over her inability to provide husbands for the young widows are wrapped in a tone of mockery that expresses her frustration. Such arguments are often used not to make a logical case so much as to make the recipients' thoughts and actions seem sillier than they perhaps are. Given her sense of helplessness, Naomi urges her daughters-in-law to return to their mothers' homes.

Naomi also wants Orpah and Ruth to recognize the cause of her sad circumstances. That cause lies beyond the human realm: The Lord is against her. To render it in a dynamic translation, "The LORD himself has raised his

---

37. Murray D. Gow, *The Book of Ruth* (Leicester: Apollos, 1992), 35.
38. Bush, *Ruth-Esther*, 78.

fist against me!" (1:13 NLT). Would these two relatively young women wish to throw in their lot with someone so ill-favored? Of course not! Although the translation of this verse can vary due to a strange syntax in Hebrew,[39] what seems certain is that Naomi is complaining about her own bitterness, which is brought upon her by the hand of the Lord.

As Hubbard notes, the hand of the Lord in the OT stands for the irresistible power of the Lord, the power that routed the mighty Philistines (1 Sam 5:9, 11), empowered fearful Elijah (1 Kgs 18:46), and comforted distressed Ezra (Ezra 7:9, 28). He observes further that whenever the "hand of the LORD" was used to express the Lord's opposition, the OT says, "The hand of the LORD *was* against [a certain person/enemy]" (Deut 2:15; Judg 2:15; 1 Sam 7:13; etc.). In Naomi's speech, however, she has substituted "was" with "turned" (literally, "went out").[40] Therefore, Naomi has first assumed that her misfortune was an attack of the Lord against her, and then postulated that this attack has far more force than the historic attacks that the hand of the Lord carries out. Now, if all her misfortune was because the hand of the Lord has courted enmity with her, the famine, the exodus to Moab, the death of her husband, and the loss of her sons are just a beginning to all the misfortune that is yet to come.

This argument, although clearly an exaggeration, could have been a very real belief in the mind of Naomi, given the multiple calamities that have piled up one after the other. In addition, if the Mediterranean cultures resemble the Indian cultures in their theology of evil, a misfortune that is brought upon individuals because of the malicious intent of a deity can also be a scary thought for people who are associated with the individual. Traditional Hindus would describe someone like Naomi as a victim of *Shani*, the god of bad luck, and would avoid partnering with them in critical matters such as business or marriage. This, therefore, is perhaps the most potent argument that Naomi uses to dissuade her daughters-in-law from following her.

Some readers may find it puzzling that Naomi declares that Yahweh is her personal adversary and yet blesses others using his name (1:9). Indians readily resign themselves to a higher power, whether beneficent or malevolent. Perhaps this attitude helps us reconcile Naomi's two speeches. In a similar manner, the

---

39. Here it is not clear whether Naomi is talking about her bitterness on account of the daughters-in-law (perhaps on account of what happened to the young ladies; *min* causal), or her bitterness as compared to that of the daughters-in-law (*min* comparative), or her bitterness as being too big to share with the daughters-in-law (*min* elative). See, Bush, *Ruth-Esther*, 80.
40. Hubbard, *The Book of Ruth*, 112–113.

Israelite is able to hold together the ideas that both blessing and curse come from Yahweh. Is this resignation to the whimsical actions of an arbitrary deity, as Indians understand their gods to be? Is this submission to the mysterious workings of a sovereign God who knows best? Is this a logical fallout of Naomi's unfaithfulness to Yahweh and his law? Whether Naomi understands Yahweh as arbitrary or sovereign or just we cannot say, but it is clear that in placing Yahweh as her adversary, she is stating a reality as she perceives it rather than making an accusation.

At any rate, this line of argumentation persuades Orpah, as much as it would persuade many of us. So Orpah is hardly to be faulted if she bids her mother-in-law of ten years a tearful farewell. As commentators note, the narrator does not make any negative evaluation of Orpah. Nevertheless, he uses her action as a foil for Ruth's action that follows. A parallel case is that of the sisters Martha and Mary. Both choose well, but one chooses better (Luke 10:41–42). As for Ruth, her choice is all the more remarkable and commendable because it is made against Naomi's impassioned argument and in contrast with Orpah's common sense decision. The two Moabites, who have been speaking and acting in unison (1:9–10) until this point, are now differentiated.

Ruth, unlike her sister-in-law, remained unconvinced by Naomi's persuasion. Therefore, while she places her arms around Naomi, she does not kiss her goodbye. As Ruth "clung" to her mother-in-law, she seems to be exhibiting a covenant commitment to Naomi which goes beyond cultural expectations. The Hebrew verb *dbq* ("cling"), which is used here to describe Ruth's action, is the same verb used in Genesis 2:24 to describe a man's action in being "united to his wife" upon getting married. The revolutionary idea there is that the woman is now his flesh and blood, literally, bone and flesh (Gen 2:23) – that is, equivalent to his kin. As such, she is not merely someone from another family who has only recently entered his and he has the same obligations to her as he would towards his blood relations. Here, similarly, Ruth is proving wrong the adage "blood is thicker than water." Even for a kinship-based society, where the "extended family was the basic unit of social and economic organization"[41] we should see Ruth as showing an extraordinarily high degree of familial loyalty towards Naomi – rather than simply towards her dead husband. By refusing to obey Naomi, she shows "loyal opposition"[42] of the kind that Moses

---

41. Davis and Parker, *Who Are You, My Daughter?*, 5.
42. Dharamraj, *A Prophet like Moses?*, 153. See George W. Coats, "The King's Loyal Opposition: Obedience and Authority in Exodus 32–34," in *Canon and Authority: Essays in Old Testament Religion and Theology*, eds. George W. Coats and Burke O. Long (Philadelphia: Fortress, 1977),

is celebrated for in the incident of the golden calf – where he will not move aside to let Yahweh visit destruction on idolatrous Israel (Exod 32:10–14).

But well beyond this, "to cling" is also how a faithful Israelite is to behave towards his God as a demonstration of his covenantal fidelity: "It is the LORD your God you must follow, and him you must revere. Keep his commands and obey him; serve him and hold fast ["cling"] to him" (Hebrew, Deut 13:5 [EV 13:4]; see also 10:20; 11:22; 30:20). The narrator could be preparing the reader for the declaration of loyalty that Ruth, like a model proselyte, will shortly make to the Israelite Naomi and to Naomi's God.[43]

1:15–18 The Third Exchange

As the figure of Orpah dwindles into the distance, we turn our attention to Ruth. Naomi makes one last attempt, this time using Orpah as a model. Twice in this verse (in the Hebrew), Naomi refers the departing sister-in-law as "your sister-in-law" – once at the beginning and once at the end: "See, your sister-in-law has gone back to her people and to her gods; return after your sister-in-law" (1:15 ESV). Naomi attempts to remind Ruth of her relationship with Orpah and tries to persuade Ruth to follow her sister-in-law's example. She begins her speech with "look." This is undoubtedly an attempt to turn Ruth's attention away from Naomi to the departing sister-in-law. Ruth, we recall, is a descendant of Lot. Lot's wife, on leaving the city of Sodom, can't resist looking back (Gen 19:17, 26). Ruth, even if entreated to "look" back, will not.[44]

Naomi's statement reminds Ruth that Orpah's return to the parental home served not just the purpose of finding security for herself (compare 1:8–9) but also demonstrated her allegiance to "her people and her gods." Therefore, Naomi appeals to Ruth's sense of loyalty towards her own people and her gods, in order to turn Ruth away from herself and to ensure that Ruth returns to Moab. In our twenty-first-century world – where national, cultural, and religious identities appear to be increasingly polarizing people – we can feel the weight of Naomi's appeal to Ruth, to choose between an old family member – who is in great pain and who has barely any promise of reciprocating the kindness she receives – and the pride of national and religious identity that would perhaps readily receive people's applause, in addition to providing security for Ruth.

91–109.

43. Davis and Parker, *Who Are You, My Daughter?*, 23.

44. LaCocque, *Ruth*, 53.

Orpah has returned to where she really belongs, her community. As in India, the community is defined by the two parameters of ethnicity and religion – "her people and her gods" (1:15). To understand the difference between these two elements of a community, we could use the example of a Kashmiri Muslim community and a Keralite Muslim community. The "gods" are the same, but the regional sociocultural variations make them thoroughly different people groups. If Ruth was going to follow Naomi to Bethlehem, she would have to negotiate a change in *both* elements of community – people and god. What sense does it make, Naomi seems to ask Ruth, to choose the double disadvantage of an unfamiliar people group that worships a different deity?[45]

We may wonder why Naomi actively encourages her daughters-in-law to return to the worship of gods other than Yahweh. In this period, the dominant understanding about gods was that each nation or people group had its high god. Moab's chief god was Chemosh, Ammon's was Milcom (see 1 Kgs 11:7), and the Canaanite peoples had Baal and his consort Asherah. Israel had Yahweh. Naomi fits into this belief system in which community and religion are a package deal.

This throws the right kind of light by which to read Ruth's speech (1:16–17). This is her first speech independent of Orpah, so it gives us a good idea of who Ruth is. Like Naomi's, Ruth's speech is a beautifully structured piece of rhetoric. In effectiveness of argumentation, it is even a notch superior to Naomi's. Whereas Naomi failed to persuade Ruth with three passionate exhortations of varying lengths, the younger woman overwhelms her mother-in-law with one comeback! The adversative conjunction "but" that begins the verse in English fulfills the same function in the same position in Hebrew. This conjunction, together with the particle of negation "Don't" that begins Ruth's speech,[46] prepares the readers for Ruth's negation of all the logic and appeal that Naomi has put forward so far. Here Ruth charges her mother-in-law not to urge her to leave Naomi or to turn back from her. As Pressler observes, the sixfold use of "you" in this verse, along with two more occurrences of this word in the following verse, show that all of Ruth's affection and attention are fixed firmly on Naomi.

Ruth's first speech comprises five couplets (1:16–17):[47]

45. Here, Brenner makes a minority position argument that it was disadvantageous for Ruth to remain in Moab. Athalya Brenner, "From Ruth to the 'Global Woman': Social and Legal Aspects," *Int* 64, no. 2 (2010): 162–168, here, 163.
46. Both in Hebrew and in English.
47. Modified from Block, *Judges, Ruth*, 640.

A	Don't urge me to leave you or to turn back from you.	Appeal to Naomi
B	Where you go I will go, and where you stay I will stay.	Ruth and Naomi
X	Your people will be my people, and your God my God.[48]	Ruth, Naomi, Yahweh
B'	Where you die I will die, and there I will be buried.	Ruth and Naomi
A'	May the LORD deal with me, be it ever so severely, if even death separates you and me.	Appeal to Yahweh

Or, alternatively, A' may be split into two parts:

| A' | May the LORD deal with me, be it ever so severely, | Appeal to Yahweh |
| | if even death separates you and me | Conclusion |

Ruth's determination to cast her lot with her Israelite mother-in-law finds expression in the matching pair B–B'. In B, Ruth uses a poetic device called *merism*, in which a poet mentions two opposites or extremes (e.g., "heaven and earth" in Gen 1:1) in order to talk about everything in between. Here Ruth uses the two opposite verbs "going" and "staying" in order to talk about a whole range of actions that are done between "going" and "staying."[49] This is a way of talking about every movement or action in life. If B speaks of circumstances that concern life, B' speaks of circumstances that concern death. Ruth vows to even die where Naomi dies, and to be buried in the same place as Naomi would be buried. This reference to burial with Naomi indicates that Ruth "considers herself a part of Naomi's family and is determined to be buried in the same family tomb."[50]

Ruth's final line could be rendered in either of two ways: (a) If the Hebrew particle *ki* is read as conditional, then: "May the LORD deal with me, be it ever so severely, *if even death* separates you and me" (1:17b NIV, italics added; see

---

48. Or, "Your people are my people, your God is my God."
49. Bush, *Ruth-Esther*, 82. Another point of interest here is that the word that Ruth uses for "stay" in Hebrew means to "lodge" temporarily (literally "for a night stay"). Therefore, it appears that Ruth was not expecting that Naomi would even have a place to live. This illustrates the high degree of Ruth's commitment to be with Naomi.
50. Block, *Judges, Ruth*, 641.

also KJV, ESV, NASB, NLT); (b) If *ki* is read as asseverative, that is declarative, then two separate sentences result: "May the LORD punish me severely if I do not keep my promise! *Only death* will be able to separate me from you!" (NET, italics added) or ". . . *Nothing but death* will be able to separate me from you."[51]

All four pairs of verbs – going, staying, dying, being buried – are attended by the locative, that is, by the word "where." In life and in death, Ruth and Naomi are to be located in a shared domestic space. Such an inseparable relationship is possible only if X (the middle couplet above) is realized: Ruth and Naomi endorse a common "people" and "gods" (1:15). So X becomes the crux of Ruth's decision. She is willing to adopt Israel and Yahweh so that she can continue alongside her foreign mother-in-law.

Ending this pledge of loyalty, Ruth invokes the name of the Lord, and uses an imprecatory oath formula ("May the LORD deal with me, be it ever so severely") which follows the pattern of ancient West Asian imprecatory oaths.[52] Hubbard explains that while such oaths were pronounced, "symbolic actions (e.g., the modern gesture of slashing one's finger across the throat) alluded to the slaughter of animals, an earlier part of the ceremony, and invoked a similar fate for breach of promise by the speaker."[53] Now, using such an oath formula, Ruth binds herself to Naomi even in death. The triple use of "die/death" in this verse shows Ruth's extremely strong determination to not let even death separate her from her mother-in-law.

Is this statement of loyalty directed at Naomi or Yahweh or both? In answering this question, we should remember that Ruth's speech is used *both* in the Jewish tradition, by the proselytes who vow allegiance to the Lord,[54] and in Christian and Jewish traditions, as a model for the high level of commitment that spouses need to emulate. Tradition has detected in this speech, allegiance to both deity and humans.

Those who hold that Ruth is declaring her conversion to Yahwism observe that, in the entire OT, this level of commitment is paralleled only by Abraham's commitment to following the Lord; it even seems to exceed Abraham's faithfulness in several ways.

---

51. A grammatically less probable variation on the declarative form is: ". . . *Not even death* will be able to separate me from you!" For this reading, the clause would need to be either introduced with אם or negated with לֹא. See Bush, *Ruth-Esther*, 83. This would, of course, be hyperbole, or is a reference to being buried side by side – we need to be careful here not to assume that Ruth is referring to being united with Naomi in the afterlife!
52. Bush, *Ruth-Esther*, 82.
53. Hubbard, *The Book of Ruth*, 119.
54. Nielsen, *Ruth*, 49.

Ruth stands alone; she possesses nothing. No God has called her; no deity has promised her blessing; no human being has come to her aid. She lives and chooses without a support group and she knows that the fruit of her decision may well be the emptiness of rejection, indeed of death. Consequently, not even Abraham's leap of faith surpasses this decision of Ruth's. And there is more. Not only has Ruth broken with family, country and faith, but she has also reversed sexual allegiance. A young woman has committed herself to the life of an old woman rather than to the search for a husband . . . One female has chosen another female in a world where life depends upon men. There is no more radical decision in all the memories of Israel.[55]

First, Ruth's words sound like a confession ("your God my God"). Second, her commitment involves a change of direction, one that is opposite to Orpah's; Ruth turned away from her past ties to Moabite deities. Third, while making an oath with Naomi, she appealed to the covenant name of the Lord (Yahweh) rather than using the name of the Moabite deity Chemosh or using a generic reference to God (Elohim).[56]

Similarly, Judaism reads Ruth's speech as a declaration of conversion. The book became particularly useful for a scattered Jewish people seeking to understand how they might admit interested Gentiles into the community. Considering the parallel that rabbinic Judaism saw between Ruth and Abraham (compare Gen 12:1 and Ruth 2:11), and considering Boaz's description of her motivation to leave Moab (2:12), the primary reason for the Jewish community to accept a convert was not marriage into the community but conversion into the faith. This desire to convert is tested by following Naomi's thrice uttered "return!" If the proselyte persists, like Ruth did, he passes the test (*Ruth Rabbah*[57] 2:16).[58] It is a two-step process: first, naturalization through joining the national community, followed automatically by the religious commitment – that is why Ruth orders her sentence "Your people . . . your God."[59]

---

55. Bush, *Ruth-Esther*, 85.
56. Hubbard, *The Book of Ruth*, 120.
57. *Ruth Rabbah* is a compilation of ancient rabbinic commentary on Ruth.
58. Jonathan Magonet, "Rabbinic Readings of Ruth," *European Judaism: A Journal for the New Europe* 40, no. 2 (2007): 150–157, here, 151.
59. Magonet, "Rabbinic Readings of Ruth," 152.

Rabbinic readings postulate a longer and more detailed conversation between Ruth and Naomi, from which they believe the biblical text excerpts Ruth's responses to Naomi's caveats for conversion.

The first of these caveats is that Israelite girls do not attend the circuses and theatres of the Gentiles, unlike Moabite girls, who would have no such restrictions. To this Ruth replies: "Where you go [literally, 'walk'] I will go [walk]."

Next, Naomi points out that Israelites would never stay in a house that does not have a *mezzuzah*[60] on the door. Ruth is quick to reply: "Where you stay, I will stay."

Naomi now informs Ruth that the Jewish people follow the 613 *mitzvoth* or commandments of the oral law handed down by the sages in their interpretation of the Torah, the books of the law. Ruth is undaunted and responds: "Your people will be my people."

Naomi then mentions the most important caveat – Israel worships only Yahweh; Ruth will have to give up her Moabite gods. Ruth is prepared for this ultimate commitment: "Your God [will be] my God."

But Naomi isn't finished yet. There is one last thing human beings value above all else – their life. Naomi explains that transgression of certain Jewish laws could result in capital punishment – death by stoning, burning, decapitation, or strangling, depending on the offence. Ruth is unfazed: "Where you die I will die, and there I will be buried."[61] In a culture in which much importance is attached to burial in one's homeland (see the cases of Jacob and Joseph; Gen 50:24–26; Josh 24:32), this is a burning of bridges – an irrevocable commitment.

From this hypothetical conversation the rabbis developed an entire catechism for conversion to Judaism!

However, another point of view is that Ruth is not showing evidence of conversion but rather, expressing her loyalty to Naomi. First, the language "your . . . my . . ." suggests that Ruth is expressing her attachment to Naomi.

---

60. A *mezzuzah* is an object fixed into the doorpost of a Jewish house in accordance with the instruction in Deuteronomy 6:9 to "write" the commandments of God "on the doorframes of your houses." It consists of a parchment or paper on which is written the "creedal" statement of Judaism, the *Shema* (Deut 6:4: "Hear, O Israel: The LORD our God, the LORD is one") that is placed inside a small receptacle, typically oblong and cylindrical.
61. The rabbinic sources are largely agreed on Naomi's part in this conversation, but there are variants, which we have not presented. See Magonet, "Rabbinic Readings of Ruth," 152–153. For samples of variants see Alshich, *A Harvest of Majesty*, 111–113 citing *Talmud Yebamoth* 47b; and Neusner, *Ruth Rabbah*, 80–82.

Second, consider the closest textual parallel to this dialogue when, many decades later, Ruth's great-grandson David listens to a similar speech.[62] David, like Naomi, is fleeing from catastrophe towards an unknown future. His son Absalom has staged a coup, and David is on the run. Ittai the Gittite – like Ruth, a foreigner – wishes to go with him, bringing his fighting men and their families. David dissuades him. He is already an exile from his own homeland, so why does he wish to risk his career with a dethroned king? Ittai's response is not unlike Ruth's: "As surely as the Lord lives, and as my lord the king lives, wherever my lord the king may be, whether it means life or death, there will your servant be" (2 Sam 15:21). David, like Naomi, acquiesces.

Third, compared to other confessions of faith in Yahweh by non-Israelites (e.g., Jethro, Exod 18:10–11; Rahab, Josh 2:9–11; Nebuchadnezzar, Dan 4:34–37; Darius, Dan 6:26–27), Ruth's two-liner has a different ring to it. The others focus their confessions on Yahweh; Ruth's declaration keeps the attention on a human being. At least at this point in the story, she chooses Yahweh because she first chooses Naomi. Indeed, rabbinic sources think that the only reason Naomi survived the catastrophe that befell the erring family was that she was instrumental in bringing Ruth to the faith of Israel.[63]

Fourth, structurally, the speech is framed by a dual appeal. Ruth opened her speech with an appeal to Naomi, asking Naomi not to dissuade her. She closes with an appeal to Yahweh to witness the irrevocability of her declaration. Therefore, as much as we would like to, we need not read Ruth's embrace of Naomi's people and God as evidence of a conversion into the Yahwistic faith. That evidence will come as we proceed further into the book; for now, this is, at best, a first step towards Yahweh.

Ruth's commitment in this verse is explained not merely as an emotion-driven speech but as determination – a volitional activity (1:18). In fact the Hebrew word for "determined" (literally, "to be strong" in the sense of "being firmly resolved")[64] captures the sense of Ruth's determination better than the English word. Hence, Ruth's determination to be "united" to Naomi, and in turn to follow the Lord, is shown as a strong volitional resolve coupled with emotional commitment.

Following this emotionally charged, high-intensity speech, "When Naomi realized that Ruth was determined to go with her, she stopped urging her"

62. See Katherine Doob Sakenfeld, *Ruth*, IBC (Louisville: Westminster John Knox, 2012), 24–25.
63. Alshich, *A Harvest of Majesty*, 72.
64. Bush, *Ruth-Esther*, 83.

(1:18). The sudden quietness in this verse is a powerful narrative tool. The intense speeches cease, and readers now have the opportunity to reflect retrospectively on all that has happened so far, in order to prepare for what will follow.[65] Naomi's silence will soon be interrupted by the agitated bustling and buzzing of the women who greet her on arrival in Bethlehem.[66] But, for now, we wonder whether the grief-stricken widow is returning to Bethlehem saddled with a responsibility she can ill afford to bear. Or, as in the story of the elephant and the mice (see the introduction to chapter 1), will the Moabite girl turn out to be the unexpected, unforeseen solution to the Jewish woman's desolation? We will have to wait and see.

1:19–22 ARRIVAL IN BETHLEHEM

The final section of this chapter contains another emotion-filled exchange[67] – this time, between Naomi and the townswomen. This section rounds off the chapter in more ways than one. The journey theme of the chapter concludes in this section. While the chapter opened with the family migrating from Bethlehem to the "fields of Moab," it concludes with the family's return from Moab, back to Bethlehem. But several things have changed between the beginning and end of the chapter. As Pressler observes, at the beginning of the chapter Naomi had no food but her family was intact, whereas at the end, there is food – for "the barley harvest was beginning" (1:22) – but barely any family.[68] At the beginning, it was a family of four, whereas now the family is reduced to two, with Naomi the only surviving member of the family that sojourned in Moab. At the beginning, in Naomi's words, she "went away full," but at the end she considers that she has come back "empty."

While the quietness of the previous verse still continues, Naomi's journey back home, which started in verse 6, now comes to an end. As soon as Naomi and Ruth arrive in Bethlehem, however, the silence is broken by an unexpected commotion – "the whole town was stirred" (1:19). The meaning of the Hebrew verb "stirred" is uncertain. It can mean various things, ranging from "agitation and consternation" to "delighted excitement." Many commentators agree[69] that the context here seems to suggest the latter sense (compare

65. Hubbard, *The Book of Ruth*, 121.
66. Davis and Parker, *Who Are You, My Daughter?*, 31.
67. Hubbard, *The Book of Ruth*, 125.
68. Pressler, *Joshua, Judges and Ruth*, 273.
69. Nielsen, *Ruth*, 51; Bush, *Ruth-Esther*, 95; Block, *Judges, Ruth*, 645; Hubbard, *The Book of Ruth*, 123, etc.

1 Sam 4:5; 1 Kgs 1:45 – images of jubilant shouting and cheerful, animated conversations upon the arrival of the ark of covenant, and upon Solomon's coronation).[70] This delightful commotion leads the townswomen to exclaim, "Can this be Naomi?" This exclamation may include an element of shock that Naomi has changed so much. But their question is primarily characterized by excitement that Naomi has finally returned.[71] Therefore, the commotion and the question in this verse signify a joyous welcome to a long-lost friend, neighbor, and extended family member (the towns of ancient Israel were predominantly occupied by members of the same tribe and clan). Clearly the women in the town are more excited about the return than Naomi herself. But will the excitement of welcoming back kinsfolk lead to making a place for the family in the town, and to resolving the crisis of Naomi's childlessness? Or is this a transient excitement which will soon fizzle out? We need to wait and watch how the rest of the story unfolds.

Naomi, however, does not respond with glee to the joyful commotion. The closing word of the question in verse 19 ("Naomi") seems to have caught Naomi's attention. This word, as we observed earlier, means to be "good/pleasant/lovely." Now we hear this word for the first time in a dialogue. In Eastern cultures, younger people in the family do not address the older ones by their name, so Naomi would not have heard any of the characters in the story refer to her by name. The tone of her response, however, is negative. Naomi's bitterness (1:13) does not seem to have disappeared yet.

Rabbinic sources reconstruct an imaginary dialogue among the incredulous Bethlehemite women, based on the supposition that Elimelek was a man of standing.

> "In times passed she would be carried in a palanquin, and now
>   she is walking barefoot, and yet you say, 'This is Naomi'!
> In times passed she would cloth herself in fine wool and now
>   she is clothed in rags, and yet you say, 'This is Naomi'!
> In times passed her face was ruddy with good nourishment
>   and drink, and now her face is pale with hunger, and yet
>   you say, 'This is Naomi'"?
> [At this point Naomi breaks in with:] "Do not call me Naomi, call
>   me Mara, for the Almighty has dealt very bitterly with me."[72]

---

70. Younger, *Judges and Ruth*, 426.
71. Pressler, *Joshua, Judges and Ruth*, 273.
72. Neusner, *Ruth Rabbah*, 92.

And so Naomi charges the townswomen to call her "Mara," which means "bitter" (it comes from the root *mrr*, "to be bitter"; a related word is "myrrh," described in the carol *We Three Kings of Orient Are* as a "bitter perfume" that the Magi gifted the baby Jesus).[73] As Hubbard notices, perhaps the sight of familiar places, and people brought back memories of Elimelek and her two sons, and this would certainly have stirred up Naomi's bitterness, and heightened her grief and pain.[74]

Naomi goes on to give a fourfold reason why people should call her Mara. Note the *chiasmus*, emphasizing her emotions through a pattern of repeated key words (1:20–21):[75]

A   *Shaddai* has dealt very bitterly with me

B   *Yahweh* has brought me back empty

B'   *Yahweh* has testified against/afflicted me

A'   *Shaddai* has brought calamity upon me

In her complaint, Naomi fixes the blame for her "bitterness" squarely upon God. Interestingly, she refers to God twice by his covenant name, *Yahweh* (the Lord) and twice by the name *Shaddai* ("the Almighty"). While the complaint seems to reflect Naomi's negative attitude towards God, the references to God seem to suggest that Naomi continues to bring herself under his care and providence. The use of the covenant name (Yahweh) may indicate that Naomi has not given up on the Lord. The reference to him as "the Almighty," however, seems to suggest that Naomi sees the God of Israel as the one who is in control of all human affairs. The meaning of the Hebrew word for "the Almighty" is unclear. But, as Hubbard notes, the OT regularly uses this word to represent "God's cosmic rulership" (Num 24:4, 16; Ps 68:14 [Hebrew 68:15]; Job 40:2; compare 34:12–13). Hubbard further observes that this name, "the Almighty," indicates the one who is

> by nature great and mysterious (Job 11:27), . . . dispenses bless-
> ings, promises great destinies (Gen 17:1; 28:3; 35:11; 43:14) and
> assigns fates to the wicked and the righteous (Job 27:14; 31:2).
> As a cosmic ruler, he also oversees the maintenance of justice
> (Job 8:3; 24:1; 27:2), meting out terrible punishments (Job 6:4;

---

73. Younger, *Judges and Ruth*, 426.
74. Hubbard, *The Book of Ruth*, 124.
75. John Currid, *Ruth: From Bitter to Sweet*, Welwyn Commentaries (Darlington, UK: Evangelical Press, 2012), 56.

23:16; 27:14–23; compare the terror of his voice, Ezek 1:24; 10:5). People appeal to him for legal vindication and rescue (Job 8:5; 13:3; 31:35). (Compare also his tender side, Ps 91:1).[76]

How should we read this? There are various ways to do so: complaint, resignation, or chastisement. On the one hand, Naomi is thoroughly upset with the Lord over her misfortune; on the other, she acknowledges that the Lord is in charge of her story. In fact, in complaining against God in her misfortune, Naomi stands alongside other OT giants such as Job, Jeremiah, Jonah, and the psalmists.[77] We hear echoes of Job's words of complaint in Naomi's complaint. Job says, "As surely as God lives, who has denied me justice, *the Almighty*, who has made my life *bitter*" (Job 27:2, italics added), which closely resembles Naomi's complaint. In addition, Naomi's feeling that the Lord has made her his target and attacked her finds parallel in Job 6:4: "The arrows of the Almighty are in me, my spirit drinks in their poison; God's terrors are marshaled against me."[78]

Naomi believes that her crisis is a result of the Lord afflicting her. The Hebrew word for "afflicted" means to "respond/speak against." In the OT, this word is usually used in a juridical context in the sense of testifying against someone (compare Exod 20:16; Num 25:30).[79] Since she believes that the Lord is the source of her misfortune, Naomi presumes that the Lord has made a judicial case against her, and that the Almighty has brought misfortune (literally, "evil") upon her. Therefore, if the Lord has brought this misfortune, it is only he who can resolve it. Naomi's complaint – along with the complaints of other OT characters, as well as Christ's complaint and cry of dereliction on the cross (Matt 27:46, compare Ps 22:1) – gives warrant for Christian complaint in similar situations, when the soul is overwhelmed.

A second way to read Naomi's speech is to see it as resignation. This comes readily to those in Eastern cultures. A human is helpless against deity. If deity unlooses disfavor upon an individual, the individual notes his misfortune but accepts it without resistance because deity cannot be resisted. Deity can only be appeased into turning away wrath.

While either complaint or resignation might be legitimate, neither reflects an entirely true reading of Naomi's situation. Her going away *full* is not entirely

76. Hubbard, *The Book of Ruth*, 125.
77. Pressler, *Joshua, Judges and Ruth*, 273.
78. Younger, *Judges and Ruth*, 427–428.
79. Younger, *Judges and Ruth*, 427.

true; neither is her coming back *empty*. Although it is true that when she had left she had all her family members with her, we cannot ignore the fact that they had migrated to Moab in the midst of hunger and famine,[80] while she is now returning to Bethlehem at the time of the barley harvest (1:22), a time of abundance of grain. Even if we interpret Naomi's fullness and emptiness only in terms of having family with her, as she makes this speech, Naomi still has Ruth standing with her (1:19).

A third way to read this text is as Judaism interprets it – that Naomi recognizes here the chastisement of God, perhaps for trading the security of her homeland for the perils of a heathen country. The rabbis compare her to the case of an ordinary ox that the owner puts up for sale. He speaks highly of it, claiming that "it is good for ploughing" since "it drives straight furrows." The astute buyers, however, notice the stripes on its back and want to know: "If it is good for ploughing, then what are these stripes doing on its back?" That is, "Why did you have to beat it?" Naomi acknowledges her "stripes," and would rather be called what she is ("bitter") than "pleasant."[81]

At the narrative level, the fact that Naomi, despite her request, is never once called "Mara" by either the narrator or the characters could indicate that the author does not completely concur with Naomi's assessment.[82]

Whichever way one reads Naomi's emotional state, it appears that the grief of the crises that Naomi went through has inflated the "bitterness" in her mind. This is evident in the increasing length and intensity of Naomi's complaint between verse 13 and verses 20–21.[83] How might a resolution to this crisis come about?

While we are not told how the resolution for Naomi's bitterness might come about, the narrator draws attention to a crucial piece in the puzzle, something that Naomi has either missed or ignored: "Naomi returned from Moab accompanied by Ruth the Moabite, her daughter-in-law." The identity of Ruth sends out mixed signals about whether she can be part of the resolution: Ruth is a Moabite, but she is also the daughter-in-law of an Israelite. We know that Ruth has pledged her loyalty to Naomi's people, but we have to wait to see if her conduct will reflect that of a Moabite or that of an Israelite. As a daughter-in-law, Ruth could be either an asset or a liability to Naomi.

---

80. The Hebrew word for "hunger" in verse 1 means "famine" as it relates to the land/nation and "hunger" as it relates to individuals.
81. Neusner, *Ruth Rabbah*, 94.
82. An observation from my MDiv Class, SAIACS (Bangalore, 2019).
83. Gow, *The Book of Ruth*, 40.

There is a trail of clues to help the reader make guesses about Ruth's role in the story ahead, clues which a postexilic redactor seems to have planted and which a postexilic audience would have picked up immediately. These are in the form of theologically weighty words, significant particularly in a period when Deuteronomy influenced Jewish national self-understanding – that is, in the postexilic period. The first chapter of Ruth embeds into its narrative key words from Deuteronomy as well as vocabulary from the exile. At first, these words apply to Naomi. Like the exilic returnees, she is the "remnant" (*sha'ar*; 1:3, 5). As such, she is the one who takes up a "return" (*shub*; 1:6, etc.) by "going out" (*yatza*; 1:7) from Moab. If Naomi acts out the exile, it is intriguing that the Deuteronomic key words, those which describe the model practitioner of the law, are acted out by Ruth. It is Ruth who is commended for practicing *hesed* (1:8).[84] As the plot rolls out, it is she who "follows after" (*halak* and *ahare*; 1:16) Naomi.[85] It is she who does not "forsake" (*azab*; 1:16),[86] but rather does the opposite and clings to Naomi, and to Naomi's people and Naomi's God.

To the exilic returnee, the word "return" has two meanings: apart from referring to a change of geographical location, it is used regularly as an invitation to the erring Israelites to come back to Yahweh. How interesting that, at the end of the chapter, Ruth is described as "Ruth the Moabite . . . the one who *returned* from the fields of Moab" (Heb 1:22). Certainly, Ruth came from the fields of Moab, but how could she be said to have "returned" from there? She has "returned" only in the sense that the Jew returns from other lands to the land of the covenant, and from following after other gods to the worship of Yahweh. With this covenantal language buzzing around her, Ruth has displaced Naomi as the female protagonist. The reader may confidently anticipate that she will bring the complicated plot to a happy resting point, for all the clues are pointing in the direction of a fulfillment of Deuteronomy's promise to those who choose not to "forsake" the Lord: "He [Yahweh] will never . . . forsake you" (Deut 31:6).

As we close, we notice how the chapter loops back upon itself, creating a pileup of reversals, some happy and some not. The chapter started with a

---

84. In Deuteronomy, *hesed* is a key attribute of Yahweh: Deut 5:10; 7:9.
85. Deuteronomy regularly uses the phrase to "follow after" to insist that Israel must not follow after other gods (e.g., Deut 4:3; 6:14; 8:19; 11:28; 13:3; 28:14), but rather, follow after Yahweh (Deut 13:5 [English 13:4]). Here, Ruth prefers not to return to her gods, but rather, opts to make Israel's God her own.
86. Deuteronomy warns Israel against forsaking Yahweh (Deut 28:20; 29:24; 31:16–17). For the theological usage and implications of *azab*, especially in Deuteronomy, see Dharamraj, *A Prophet like Moses?*, 94–98.

journey out of Bethlehem to Moab and ends with a journey from Moab to Bethlehem. Elimelek led his family out, but Naomi leads her (remaining) family back. The number returning is half that of the number that went out. The emigrants were largely men, but the returnees are only women. The men could pride themselves on pedigree – they were Ephrathites; of the women returning, one is a despicable Moabite. This is how the Bethlehemites would see this sad turn of events.

More positively, the story began with a political time marker ("in the days when the judges ruled") that indicates cycles of increasingly destructive reigns; it finishes with an agrarian time marker ("the barley harvest was beginning") which assures us of the restoration of order in the seasonal cycles. The end of April and the beginning of May were the months for both the barley and wheat harvests. That Naomi and Ruth should arrive at this time might signal fruitfulness in the story that is yet to unfold.

The unseen actor, Yahweh, has solved the crisis that caused the migration – famine (1:6). Will he now somehow provide a resolution to the crisis caused by barrenness, the loss of males, and the consequent insecurity?

WIDOWS AND WIDOWHOOD IN THE HINDU TRADITIONS IN INDIA

The book of Ruth is a window into widowhood in ancient Israel. Here are women who live on the edges of society. They pick up the leftovers of the wealthy. Although they have legal rights, they are powerless to appropriate them. They yearn to live under the protection of a male, whether husband or son. Their outlook on life is bitterly bleak. Even God, they might think, has turned against them.

Snapshots of their pitiable condition are scattered across the canon. In the small town of Zarephath, a famine leaves a widow and her young son reconciling themselves to death by starvation. She is scrabbling for sticks with which to fuel the final meal she can provide her little family (1 Kgs 17). There is Anna, widowed at what was probably a ridiculously young age, after only seven years of marriage. We wonder if she had anyone to care for her, since we hear she spends all her days fasting and praying in the temple precincts (Luke 2:36–37). In those same precincts, while the rich are flaunting the offerings they can put into the treasury, a widow brings all she has and yet it amounts to no more than "two very small copper coins, worth only a few cents" (Mark 12:41–44). In another town in first-century Palestine, a judge attends to a widow's case only because she will not stop knocking on his door with the plea, "Grant me justice against my adversary" (Luke 18:2–5). Perhaps she is a victim of one of the "teachers of the law," who "have the most important seats in the synagogues and the places of honor at banquets" but do not bat an eyelid while they "devour widows' houses" (Mark 12:38–40). The circumstance of widowhood is the image that comes readily to the poet as he describes Jerusalem fallen to the Babylonian invader, looted and stripped: "How deserted lies the city, once so full of people! How like a widow is she, who once was great among the nations! . . . Bitterly she weeps at night, tears are on her cheeks" (Lam 1:1–2).

Within some Hindu communities of central and northern India, there was a time when the death of a man meant that his widow should get ready to immolate herself on his funeral pyre. The practice was called *sati* and was seen as the highest statement a woman could make about her devotion to her (deceased) husband. Even though it was banned in 1829 under British rule and was further legislated against in 1987 in independent India, there are still sporadic reports of the practice.

More pervasive across India are the negative attitudes towards widows. First, a widow is expected to spend the remainder of her life in mourning for her husband. Such an existence entails staying as unattractive as possible, and so she is forbidden jewelry. A common funeral ritual for the man includes the elimination of all markers of a married woman – the vermillion that dots the forehead (*sindoor*), the black-beaded necklace (*mangalasutra*), and the toe rings. Her (glass) bangles are ceremonially broken, symbolizing the end of her life as a married woman. To prevent her from appearing attractive to men, her head could be shaved, and she would be required to stay in that state for the rest of her life. From this point on, she wears no makeup and dresses as plainly as possible, usually in white. In fact, white is so closely associated with widowhood that it is traditionally considered inauspicious for anyone but a widow to wear it on a celebratory occasion. To keep her libido in check, her diet is now restricted. Meat is removed, along with certain vegetables, and the frequency of her meals may be reduced to once a day.

A second, and far more serious, perspective on widowhood is to lay the blame for the man's death on his widow. She is considered to be ill-omened and hence to be avoided. She may be isolated by being confined to a room in the house; she may be treated as an "untouchable" – one whose contact brings bad luck – and so required to cover her face with a veil (*ghoonghat*) when in public because of the belief that even the sight of her bodes ill. If ever she should marry again, she is sure to pass on the "jinx" to her new husband – rather like the story of Tamar, in which Judah was afraid that he might lose his third son to her (Gen 38:11). The widow must not only deal with her grief at being bereaved, but also carry the staggering weight of guilt at having somehow brought about her husband's death. With all this comes a deep sense of shame, not to be taken lightly in a South Asian culture.

A third aspect of widowhood in India, flowing from the two points discussed above, is the stripping of identity. Since a woman's identity traditionally derives from that of the husband, a widow ceases to have a place in society. Some communities go further, dehumanizing the widow by referring to her with the gender-neutral pronoun "it." She is, as one Indian psychologist put it, "physically alive but socially dead."[1] She may not have any right to inherit property. With no husband to support her needs, she is passed into the hands of a son or a male relative, who might see her as an economic burden. From here, she is

---

1. Megan Palin, "The Mysterious Place Where Thousands of Widows Flock to Live," *News.com.au*, accessed February 17, 2018, https://www.news.com.au/world/asia/the-mysterious-place-where-thousands-of-widows-flock-to-live/news-story/6bef3703bdcac89ca811fc7e457f2ccf.

only a step away from being abandoned. Vrindavan – called "the city of widows" – and Varanasi are (in)famous as places for unwanted widows. These women often live in shelters, supposedly withdrawn into a life of prayer, begging at temples to fend off starvation, and, if they are young, finding themselves forced into prostitution.

Against these dismal descriptions of what *is* are shining prescriptions of what *should be*. The OT law offers special protection for the widow, forbidding that anyone should "take advantage" of her: "If you do and they cry out to me, I will certainly hear their cry. My anger will be aroused, and I will kill you with the sword; your wives will become widows and your children fatherless" (Exod 22:22–24). The intention of the levirate legislation was that a widow should never be without a family; the purpose of the gleaning laws for grain, olives, and grapes was that a widow living on her own would not go hungry; the widow in dire straits would always (at least) keep warm at night since a debtor could never foreclose on her cloak (Deut 2:17). In the agricultural cycle, a special tithe in the third year of harvest was meant to be gathered in and then distributed to, among others, the widow (Deut 14:28–29; 26:12–13). One who exploited the helplessness of a widow came under the disfavor of God: "Cursed is anyone who withholds justice from . . . the widow" (Deut 27:19). The prophets never failed to include the cause of the widow in their rebuke of corruption in the social order (Isa 1:17; 10:2; Jer 7:6; 22:3; Ezek 22:7; Zech 7:10; Mal 3:5).

Israel's God described himself as "a defender of widows" (Ps 68:5; compare Deut 10:18). He invites them to "depend on me" (Jer 49:11) since he is committed to "sustain[ing]" them (Ps 146:9). We see this acted out in Jesus's ministry. When Jesus ran into the funeral procession of a widow's only son, his "heart went out to her," and he raised to life the one who was her security (Luke 7:12–15). As the time of his death approached, Jesus committed his widowed mother into the care of John (John 19:26–27). The early church stayed faithful to this mandate of God, taking seriously the support of widows among them (Acts 6:1–5; 1 Tim 5:3; Jas 1:27).

Against this commentary on widows and widowhood in ancient Israel, first-century Palestine, and present-day India, the significance of a pair of widows cast as the protagonists of a biblical book is not to be missed. It calls for a seismic shift in social paradigm and worldview to appreciate the place of these two widows in God's great scheme for the salvation of humankind, for Ruth will have a place in the earthly ancestry of Jesus.

Havilah Dharamraj

RUTH 2

An Indian folktale tells of a king on a war march, needing grain to feed his army. Stopping outside a village, the king ordered his commander to find food. The commander went ahead on the road, and soon encountered a farmer. "Show me the largest field hereabouts," he ordered. The farmer took him to a field ripe with wheat. "Right! I'll harvest this grain," the commander said. The farmer was taken aback. "Oh, not this one, sir!" he pleaded. "I'll show you another one." The farmer led the soldiers to another field, smaller but just as plentiful. Once the crop had been harvested, the commander asked the farmer why he had led them to this particular field. "This is my field, sir," the farmer responded. "I couldn't have allowed you to take what is someone else's without putting up resistance. But I'm happy to let you have what is mine, especially since you are fighting a war to keep us safe." The king, on hearing about this farmer's generosity, repaid him with much wealth.

The second chapter of the book of Ruth tells about kind deeds, and about people who are happy to share what is theirs, whether they have much or little. We shall see these deeds of thoughtful generosity as we follow one day in the life of Ruth as a new immigrant in the little town of Bethlehem.

STRUCTURE

Ruth and Naomi have negotiated the long and dangerous journey across the mountain range and the Dead Sea valley that separate Moab from Israel. But now, in Bethlehem, the questions of immediate survival and future hope remain. This chapter takes the plot a step further towards the resolution of these questions. Resolution happens by way of multiple "coincidences, blessings and human acts of . . . kindness," all of which "point to the hidden activity of God."[1]

Set in the harvest-fields of Bethlehem, chapter 2 is dominated by the verb "to glean." The legally mandated practice of gleaning allowed the poor to pick up the crumbs that fell from the rich man's table. Here in Bethlehem, the rich man has a face – that of Boaz. Boaz is the third and last of the story's protagonists to enter the scene.

As with chapter 1, chapter 2 may be neatly spliced by location. If, in the opening chapter, the story moved from Bethlehem to Moab and back to

---

1. Pressler, *Joshua, Judges and Ruth*, 275.

Bethlehem, in the second chapter, the movement is local. The scenes shift from within a home (2:2) to out in the fields (2:3–17) and back to the home (2:18–22), moving seamlessly between the private and the public. Framing these scenes are the storyteller's asides to us, the readers (2:1, 23).

Just as well-ordered as the structure is the sequence of events – it depicts a typical working day in harvesttime, moving from morning (2:7) to midday (2:14) to evening (2:17). Within this setting, the storyteller executes a creative version of the cinematic strategy of "upstairs-downstairs"[2] by shifting the point of view: first, we see through the eyes of destitute women; next, we are at the opposite end of the economic spectrum, seeing from a wealthy landowner's perspective; and then we are returned to the women. Besides the binary pairs of male/female and rich/poor, we also have – especially as Ruth comes face-to-face with Boaz – old/young and Judahite/foreigner.[3]

As if all this wasn't enough, the storyteller sneaks in an admirable arrangement of conversation groups:

A   2:2: Ruth and Naomi
B   2:4–7: Boaz and the reapers
X   2:8–14: Boaz and Ruth
B'   2:15–16: Boaz and the reapers
A'   2:19–22: Ruth and Naomi[4]

With this, the storyteller has made the first meeting of his lead actor and actress the centerpiece of the chapter and allocated to them the longest dialogue. The plot moves from Ruth's tentative foray into gleaning to two full harvests with gleaning privileges assured; from emptiness to fullness; from vulnerable to protected; from hopelessness to possibility. Based on this structure, the turning point is undoubtedly the encounter between Boaz and Ruth.

2:1 OPENING NOTE

Indian cinema expends a great deal of energy on the entry of the male protagonist, especially if the movie star in question is popular. There is the long

---

2. This schema is popularized, for example, in the television series *Downton Abbey* and in the movie *Viceroy's House*, where an event is seen through the dual lens of master and servant, rich and poor.
3. Tod Linafelt, *Ruth: Studies in Hebrew Narrative and Poetry*, Berit Olam (Collegeville, MN: Liturgical Press, 1999), 23.
4. Modified mildly from LaCocque, *Ruth*, 60.

buildup which climaxes in a dramatic introduction of the hero, whereupon the theater audience bursts into animated cheering, punctuated with wolf whistles.

Boaz, too, makes a dramatic entry. The buildup is the lengthy opening sentence which tells us about a certain relative of Naomi's. Only the last word discloses the identity of this relative – Boaz. Even as we wonder about the relevance of this information, the plot places Ruth in a field belonging to Boaz (2:3). Fast on the heels of that connection enters the man himself (2:4). Let's look at the note that introduces his name (2:1).

First, the narrator tells us that this man is Naomi's "relative on her husband's side." Although some scholars believe that the Hebrew word *moda*[5] ("relative") should be translated "friend/acquaintance,"[6] it is apt to translate this word as "relative" – someone who belongs to the extended family of Naomi's husband. The same Hebrew word occurs elsewhere in the Hebrew Bible in conjunction with other familial terms (Prov 7:4). Additionally, the book of Ruth lays emphasis on Boaz being a "guardian-redeemer" (*goel*; 2:20; 3:9, 12) which is very much a function of someone who is a blood relative.[7] This blood relative, as this verse discloses, is on Naomi's husband's side. This is an important piece of information, especially given that Israelite marriages were commonly endogamous, that is, within the extended family or clan.[8]

Second, the narrator tells us that this new character is "a man of standing" (*ish gibbor hayil*). This Hebrew term can also be translated with a military sense as a "mighty man of valor," "noble warrior," or "military hero."[9] However, given the farming context, the role that Boaz eventually plays in the story, and the use of a similar term in Proverb 31:10 to describe a woman of noble character, we gather that this "man of standing" is a man of noble character, respected by the members of his community. The phrase could also indicate a "man of (material) substance." This is perhaps how the angel addresses Gideon, the son of a wealthy landowner in Oprah (Judg 6:12).[10] In an Indian village, such a person of character and substance would be elected to the *gram panchayat*, the

5. The *ketiv* spelling is probably defective: מְיָדַע. The *kere* corrects it to מוֹדַע. Rabbinic comment sees possible significance in the *yod* of the *ketiv*. The *yod* may be a short-hand reference to Yahweh, "as if to allude to the fact that besides a relative, there was God too . . ."; Alshich, *A Harvest of Majesty*, 138.
6. Hubbard, *The Book of Ruth*, 132.
7. See Block, *Judges, Ruth,* 650–651; Bush, *Ruth-Esther*, 100.
8. Bush, *Ruth-Esther*, 100.
9. Block, *Judges, Ruth*, 651.
10. Other occurrences are: 1 Sam 9:1; 1 Kgs 11:28; 2 Kgs 15:20. Considering the particular context of the Gideon story, it is possible that two senses of the Hebrew term – "wealthy man" and "mighty warrior" – are layered over each other.

council that arbitrates in local cases. We see that Boaz is qualified to perform a similar function when he summons a meeting of Bethlehem's elders (4:2).

From the Midrash comes a proleptic association: the phrase is also applicable to David, though in the military sense, since Saul takes into his employment "mighty" men (*ish gibbor*) and "brave" warriors (*ben hayil*) (1 Sam 14:52).[11] David has a worthy ancestor in Boaz! Along these lines is the *Ruth Rabbah*, a compilation of ancient rabbinic commentary. Working out David's pedigree from the standing of Boaz and Ruth, the rabbis remark: "If a giant marries a giantess [w]hat do they produce? Mighty men of valour." Thus: "Boaz married Ruth and whom did they produce? David: 'Skilful in playing, and a mighty man in valor, and a man of war, prudent in affairs, good-looking, and the Lord is with him' (1 Sam 16:18)."[12]

Third, we are told that this man is from the clan of Elimelek. The Hebrew word for "clan" most probably indicates a subdivision of a tribe.[13] As Bush observes, this is probably the most organized kinship group and the most basic endogamous unit of the society.[14] The clan is a "cluster of households related by blood and marriage" which, "provided some degree of social cohesion, offering protection to its weaker members and laying obligation upon the stronger ones."[15]

With each added descriptor, this new character holds increasing promise for the future of Naomi and Ruth: he is a blood relative, he is wealthy, he is the dead Elimelek's close kin.

Rounding off this string of information with a flourish is the name itself: Boaz. Scholars have interpreted the meaning of this name variously: (i) it is possibly linked to the Arabic *baġz*, "to be vigorous, strong of spirit"; (ii) it derives from the Hebrew *Booz* (as the Septuagint transliterates this word) which is perhaps an abbreviation of *bĕ'ōz yhwh*, "in the strength of Yahweh [I will rejoice/trust]";[16] and (iii) it is the same meaning as the name of the pillar called *Boaz*, one of a pair that will later stand in Solomon's temple (1 Kgs 7:21),[17] signifying strength. Whatever the etymology of the name, it has positive associations. Yet, there is a negative undercurrent. As Sakenfeld points out, Boaz's wealth and standing places him at the opposite end of the

---

11. LaCocque, *Ruth*, 62.
12. Neusner, *Ruth Rabbah*, XXVII:i.2.
13. Block, *Judges, Ruth*, 651.
14. Bush, *Ruth-Esther*, 101.
15. Davis and Parker, *Who Are You, My Daughter?*, 39.
16. Block, *Judges, Ruth*, 651.
17. Pressler, *Joshua, Judges and Ruth*, 276.

social spectrum to this pair of impoverished widows. (This divide will later collapse when Boaz – the *ish gibbor hayil* – identifies Ruth as a "worthy woman" – *esheth hayil*; 3:11.)[18]

The question this note in 2:1 introduces is this: What role will the praiseworthy Boaz play? There is a happy anticipation set up by the order of names:

the living (kinsman) – the dead (Elimelek) – the living (Boaz)

Perhaps the living will restore the fortunes of the dead. A short panel structure can be discerned in the verse:[19]

A   Naomi's relative

    B   Man of standing

A'   Elimelek's clan

    B'   Boaz

2:2 AT HOME

Having broken the narrative frame to favor the reader with information that the characters are yet to encounter, the storyteller now returns to the story. Knowing more than the three actors know, we enjoy the anticipation building up in the events that follow as they ask each other questions and piece together bits of information. It is a brilliant narrative strategy. Twenty-first century readers are accustomed to the opposite – to suspense, in which the storyteller *withholds* information. In Ruth we shall see that prior knowledge of the plot can draw in the reader just as much as suspense does.

Unlike chapter 1, in which Naomi is the primary actor with Ruth responding to Naomi's initiatives, here the situation is reversed. Ruth's decisive actions drive the plot, while Naomi responds.[20] In addition to the determination Ruth exhibited in the previous chapter, she now shows resourcefulness. As a new immigrant venturing into public space, she will need both. The verb Ruth uses both earlier and now is the same: "go" (*halak*; 1:18; 2:2). But instead of the familiar and fruitful "fields [sg. *sadeh*] of Moab" (1:6), she ventures now into the potentially hostile "fields" (sg. *sadeh*) of a foreign country.

18. Sakenfeld, *Ruth*, 38.
19. Francis Matthew, "Exegesis of Ruth," MDiv Class, SAIACS (Bangalore, 2019).
20. In 2:2, in the Hebrew, the 10-word long speech of Ruth elicits a 21-word response from Naomi, each word no more than three letters in length.

The destitute stave off starvation by gleaning, and it is to keep the pair of widows alive that Ruth politely seeks the older woman's permission to try her luck in the fields. In reporting this conversation, the narrator refers to Ruth's ethnicity – she is "Ruth the Moabite" (2:2). Perhaps this is to highlight the extraordinary nature of Ruth's action.[21] Here is a Moabite hoping to glean in an Israelite field. Gleaning was probably well established in ancient West Asian legal provisions for the care of socially vulnerable people.[22] A possible resemblance to the Israelite sanction on gleaning could be found in the twenty-eighth chapter of *The Instruction of Amen-em-opet*, with a very specific reference to the widows being the beneficiary.[23]

The Israelite law code makes specific provisions for economically disadvantaged persons – widows, orphans, resident aliens – to "pick up the leftover grain" (literally, "to glean, to gather scraps") from the fields of the Israelites. There were three kinds of leftovers. First, the stalks of grain that fell down in the process of reaping the harvest and bundling into sheaves were to be left for the poor (Lev 19:9; 23:22). Second, even if the reapers left a whole sheaf behind in the field by oversight, they were not to go back to retrieve it (Deut 24:19). The third regulation was more intentional: the reapers were to deliberately refrain from reaping right up to the edges of the field, leaving these peripheral strips for the needy to harvest (Lev 19:9; 23:22). Davis and Parker point out that, in this chapter, the verb "to glean" is a motif-word, occurring a good dozen times (2:2, 3, 7, 8, 15–19, 23) and always with Ruth as the subject.[24] Perhaps the repetitions are to establish her as someone who well fits the category for whom the gleaning laws were mandated – in one sense or another, she is an orphan, a widow, and a stranger (Deut 24:19)[25] – and that she is under the protection of Israelite law.[26] This anticipates the levirate and property redemption laws that will elevate her to full and dignified membership within the community. Indeed, this book robustly affirms the potential of the Israelite legal code to act in favor of the less fortunate strata of society.

---

21. Block, *Judges, Ruth*, 652.
22. Nielsen, *Ruth*, 54.
23. See James B. Pritchard, ed., *Ancient Near Eastern Texts: Relating to the Old Testament*, 3rd ed. with supplement (Princeton: Princeton University Press, 1969), 424.
24. Davis and Parker, *Who Are You, My Daughter?*, 43.
25. Linafelt, *Ruth*, 27.
26. Davis and Parker, *Who Are You, My Daughter?*, 43. For a nuanced reading of the gleaning rights of the Moabite Ruth, see Agnethe Siquans, "Foreignness and Poverty in the Book of Ruth: A Legal Way for a Poor Foreign Woman to Be Integrated into Israel," *JBL* 128, no. 3 (2009): 443–452.

Nevertheless, either because the implementation of the gleaning laws was being neglected,[27] or because Ruth the foreigner is unsure of being accommodated, or both, Ruth deems it appropriate to glean only "behind anyone in whose eyes I find favor." As Block points out, the expression "to find favor in N's eyes" is the language of law court settings, "where subjects would acknowledge their dependence upon and need for grace at the hands of the king or judge." Given this, "[i]f the favour of the superior cannot be taken for granted under normal circumstances, how much less when the supplicant is a widowed alien, and when the spiritual condition of the Israelites is as low as it is portrayed in the book of Judges?"[28] It is also significant that this phrase appears about thirteen times in the OT to describe a person's position before God (see Exod 33:13; Judg 6:17).[29] We will see how cleverly the narrator overlaps the roles of God and Boaz to make his point that humans are mediators of divine providence. Sometimes, these mediators are well-resourced – like Barzillai who provisioned the camp of David as he fled into self-exile (2 Sam 17:27–29; 19:32). At other times, those who provide barely have enough for themselves. Such was the case of the widow at Zarephath, who took in Elijah at a time of drought (1 Kgs 17:8–16). In our story, Ruth's reference to a provider – "anyone in whose eyes I find favor" – turns out to be an unwitting proleptic reference to Boaz.[30]

Ruth hopes for favor from the Bethlehemite farming community, but it is possible that the injunction against alliances with Moabites (Deut 23:3–6) could be (unfairly) used against her.[31] So Ruth cannot be certain that her foray will be successful. She must find a reaper who will not hustle her off his master's field. In contrast to Ruth's feisty optimism in the face of such uncertainty, the terseness of Naomi's response may suggest that a sense of hopelessness continues to overwhelm her.[32]

---

27. Note that in the time of the judges, "everyone did as they saw fit" (Judg 17:6; 21:25; compare Ruth 1:1). A similar situation arises in a later period in Israelite history, when the prophets have to remind landowners of their obligations to the needy (Amos 5:10–15; Mic 3:1–3; Isa 1:17; 5:8–13; 18:4–6).
28. Block, *Judges, Ruth*, 118.
29. LaCocque, *Ruth*, 63.
30. Currid, *Ruth*, 66.
31. So, LaCocque, *Ruth*, 63.
32. Sakenfeld, *Ruth*, 39.

2:3–17 IN THE FIELDS

Ruth's day out takes up most of the account that follows, and can be punctuated to demarcate four episodes: Ruth's introduction to Boaz (2:3–7), followed by Boaz's first act of kindness (2:8–13), and then his second (2:14) and third (2:15–17) acts of kindness.

2:3–7 Boaz Notices Ruth

The narrator moves us from indoors to outdoors with a speedy succession of three verbs that describe Ruth's movements. In the Hebrew, she *goes out*, she *comes* to a field, and begins to *glean* (2:3). The storyteller, in another aside, gives us information of which Ruth remains ignorant. He tells us that "as it turned out, she was working in a field belonging to Boaz" (2:3). Literally, "and her chance chanced upon," or as the modern idiom would render it, "by a stroke of luck."[33] In this context, however, this stroke of luck cannot be interpreted merely as a random occurrence of chance. It could be interpreted similarly to the South Indian expression *adhrishtam* ("good fortune"). *Adhrishtam* assumes an unseen entity behind a favorable event. Similarly, Ruth's stroke of luck should be understood as divine orchestration.[34] In the book of Esther – set in the postexilic period in which the book of Ruth was possibly edited – coincidence becomes shorthand for God's interventions. For example, the insomniac king discovers that he owes Mordecai a favor just as Haman is plotting to execute Mordecai (Esth 6:1–10). Nothing happens to us that God has not scheduled into our calendar; we meet no one with whom God has not arranged an appointment for us.

In this story, Ruth ends up in Boaz's field. The narrator reminds us again that Boaz was from the clan of Elimelek. Therefore, this "chance" now opens up the faint possibility of Boaz becoming part of the resolution of Ruth and Naomi's story. Across the verses 2:1 and 2:3, there is a telling concentric arrangement of names (similar to the one noted in 2:1):

Elimelek (2:1) – Boaz (2:1) – Boaz (2:3) – Elimelek (2:3)

---

33. Block, *Judges, Ruth*, 653. מִקְרֶה can mean "fate" or "destiny" in Ecclesiastes (2:14–15; 3:19; 9:2–3); but the meaning here is probably closer to "chance" or "accident" as in 1 Samuel 6:9; 20:26.

34. Even though the book does not show God's active intervention in the turns of the plot, he is not absent in its theology. He is mentioned 23 times, twice by the narrator and the rest within the dialogue: Yahweh (17 times); Elohim (thrice for the God of Israel; once for the gods of Moab); Shaddai (twice). LaCocque, *Ruth*, 64 n. 8.

The deceased Elimelek's name fades towards the edges, while the name of Boaz bursts in to occupy central position, anticipating his crucial role in the unfolding story.

As if Ruth gleaning in Boaz's field was not coincidence enough, the narrator presents yet another incident of "chance": "Just then Boaz arrived from Bethlehem" (2:4a). In fact, the Hebrew does not even have the time descriptor "just then." It simply says, "And see! Boaz! He came from Bethlehem." This double coincidence indicates that Ruth did not just happen to be on Boaz's field, she also happened to be in a position to encounter Boaz himself.[35]

As Boaz entered the field, he greets the harvesters, "The LORD be with you!" and they respond in similar fashion, "The LORD bless you!" (2:4). These greetings are generic. A present-day example would be "goodbye," which in its original sense probably meant "God be with you," but today simply means "farewell."[36] The divine name occurs across the greetings in a chiastic placement, giving it a visual prominence in this story in which God acts behind the scenes:

Yahweh   (may he) bless you   with you   Yahweh

Placing the name of the Lord on the lips of both great (Boaz) and small (the harvesters) seems to indicate that the Lord is involved in each turn of the plot.[37]

At this point, Boaz notices Ruth. He turns to the overseer (Heb. "young man who was in charge of the reapers") and asks him "Who does that young woman belong to?" The categorization of both the overseer and Ruth as "young" introduces the possibility of another suitor for Ruth. Further, since Ruth has started gleaning in this field, it is plausible that this is because she has "found favor" (2:2) in the eyes of this foreman. Will the overseer be the man in whose home she would "find rest" (1:9), facilitated and blessed by Boaz, the "man of standing"? Or is the overseer introduced in this manner simply to keep the reader guessing? We will soon find out.

Meanwhile, we notice that Boaz's question to the overseer is literally: "Who does that young woman belong to?" This question could be a reflection of the patriarchal assumption in Boaz's society that, with the exception of the heads of the households (normally free Israelite males), all others, especially women, had their identity as persons belonging to or being in relationship with a man

---

35. Hubbard, *The Book of Ruth*, 143.
36. Pressler, *Joshua, Judges and Ruth*, 278; Sakenfeld, *Ruth*, 40.
37. Hubbard, *The Book of Ruth*, 144–145.

– "father, husband, master, or possibly brother or grown-up son."[38] A similar question – "Who do you belong to?" – is posed to male household servants elsewhere (Gen 32:17 [Hebrew 32:18]; 1 Sam 30:13), eliciting responses which give the identity of the master.[39] Here, the overseer's response is, "She is the Moabite who came back from Moab with Naomi" (2:6). This not only answers Boaz's question but draws his attention to Ruth's relationship to the line of Elimelek, highlighting Boaz's responsibility as "a relative . . . from the clan of Elimelek."[40] The overseer's mention of Ruth's Moabite ethnicity could possibly be discriminatory[41] although, given his subsequent good report of her conduct, this may not be the case. But certainly, the implication is that everyone in town knows about this Moabite who has come back with Naomi. She is the talk of the town (1:19).

The overseer continues and informs Boaz that Ruth had sought his permission to "glean and gather among the sheaves behind the harvesters." This information may help us understand why Boaz noticed Ruth almost immediately on arrival. Hubbard explains that, in Bible times, the reapers grasped the stalks with their left hand and cut them with a sickle in their right hand. Once they accumulated an armload of stalks, they would leave the bunch in rows for the women harvesters to bundle up. The women would bundle up the stalks, being careful not to leave any stalks behind. The gleaners who came after them had barely anything left to collect. Hence the fallen grains that the gleaners gathered would have provided mere subsistence living.[42] This is similar to the way rag-pickers across India make a living out of scrap and rejects.

Given the insufficiency of such gleanings to support the living of two women, it appears that Ruth has requested special permission to glean among the sheaves. Although gleaning of stalks of grain that have escaped being bundled was permitted, it is possible that gleaners were restricted from this work area till later in the day or until the sheaves were removed from the field. This would have kept the gleaners from getting in the way of those harvesting and bundling, and also prevented them from helping themselves to the sheaves. Though the overseer does not explicitly say that he has granted Ruth permission to glean between the sheaves, it is likely that he has, since she has already

38. Pressler, *Joshua, Judges and Ruth*, 279.
39. Sakenfeld, *Ruth*, 41.
40. Block, *Judges, Ruth*, 655.
41. Pressler, *Joshua, Judges and Ruth*, 279.
42. Hubbard, *The Book of Ruth*, 138.

started doing so (2:3).[43] He merely reports to his employer that: "She came into the field and has remained [literally, she 'stood'] here from morning till now." Perhaps because he had exceeded his authority, the overseer does not mention whether or not he has given Ruth the permission. Seeing this stranger among the harvesters and the sheaves, Boaz tries to find out who this young woman is. By seeking permission to glean among the sheaves, Ruth has exhibited courage and initiative to meet her family's needs; perhaps, unwittingly, she has also given Boaz an opportunity to notice her.

Rabbinic remarks take a different route to establish why Ruth caught Boaz's eye. "Since [Boaz] saw her as such a proper woman, whose deeds were so proper, he began to ask about her." What were these proper deeds?

> "All the other women bend down to gather gleanings, but this
>   one sits down and gathers.
> "All the other women hitch up their skirts. She keeps
>   hers down.
> "All the other women make jokes with the reapers. She
>   is modest.
> "All the other women gather from between the sheaves [and the grain
>   there is not in the category of gleanings]. She gathers only from
>   the grain that has already been left behind."[44]

While some Christian commentators speculate that Ruth courageously asked to glean beyond the allowance of the law, ancient rabbinic commentary sees her as praiseworthy for keeping the law. At any rate, Ruth catches the eye of the landowner for reasons that do her credit.

The overseer concludes with a phrase (2:7) unclear in the Hebrew. Some of the more common renderings are:[45] (i) "She . . . has remained here from morning till now, *except for a short rest in the shelter*" (NIV, italics added); (ii) ". . . without resting even for a moment" (NRSV), following the Septuagint's "she has not rested in the field"; and (iii) ". . . she has been sitting in the [shelter] for a little while" (NASB). Whether Ruth has rested briefly or not, the

---

43. Verse 3a need not be considered as a summary statement of the entire day as Bush and Hubbard suggest (Bush, *Ruth-Esther*, 104; Hubbard, *The Book of Ruth*, 140), since it only consists of three actions of Ruth ("go," "enter," and "glean"), out of which the first two are of very little significance to the rest of the story, whereas 3a excludes several other significant actions of the day that would be expected in a summary statement.
44. Neusner, *Ruth Rabbah*, XXXI:i.2.
45. For possible variant renderings, see Block, *Judges, Ruth*, 657–658; Sakenfeld, *Ruth*, 42.

sense in all these translations is that the overseer has noticed, with approval, Ruth's diligence.

Here we pause to take note of the setting in which Boaz and Ruth meet. Alter famously introduced the idea of type scenes in Hebrew narrative, providing as an example the theme of boy-meets-girl-at-well.[46] Thus Jacob first sees Rachel at a well for watering herds (Gen 29:1–12). Moses meets Zipporah and her sisters at a Midianite well (Exod 2:15–22). A variation on the theme is Rebekah meeting her future husband's emissary Eliezer at the town well (Gen 24:11–18). A subtle twist on the type scene is Tamar waiting to trick her trickster father-in-law Judah at the entrance to the city of Enaim ("wells" or "springs"; Gen 38:14). Boaz meets Ruth in a fertile field, which in itself promises a reversal of her barrenness. But cunningly woven into the setting is the type scene motif, anticipating that Boaz and Ruth will not only marry each other but also become a celebrity couple. In his very first address to Ruth, Boaz invites her to help herself to a drink anytime she is thirsty (2:9). While the stage setting may not include a well, there are props to compensate – water jars!

2:8–13 Boaz's First Act of Kindness

Boaz now performs a series of three acts of kindness, the first of which is captured entirely within a dialogue.

In keeping with the social distance between Boaz and Ruth, Boaz initiates a conversation with Ruth. He starts his speech with "My daughter, listen to me" (2:8). This is often read as indicative of a significant age difference between Boaz and Ruth. Jewish lore is fancifully specific, putting Ruth's age at forty while Boaz is made an octogenarian who had buried his wife the very day that Naomi and Ruth arrived in Bethlehem.[47] A South Asian, however, might read this very differently. In South India, females of any age could be addressed with the suffix *amma* ("mother") appended to their given name. This is simply an honorific suffix and in no way indicative of the age of the addressee. If this is the case in Ruth, then Ruth does not need to be a whole generation younger than Boaz. By calling her "daughter," Boaz seems to be communicating warmth to Ruth, breaking down the social inequality barrier between him and her.[48]

46. Robert Alter, *The Art of Biblical Narrative* (New York: Basic Books, 1981), 51–59. For a detailed exploration of the betrothal type scene showing how the Boaz–Ruth story plays it out, see Michael W. Martin, "Betrothal Journey Narratives," *CBQ* 70, no. 3 (2008): 505–523.
47. Louis Ginzberg, *The Legends of the Jews*, trans. Henrietta Szold and Paul Radin, vol. 2 (HardPress, 2016), 863–864.
48. Block, *Judges, Ruth*, 659.

Indeed, the two instructions that follow communicate Boaz's care for Ruth. First, Boaz advises Ruth not to look for other fields to glean in. The rabbis have a comment here: "There are two hundred [and] forty-eight limbs in a human being, but people follow only their eyes." This is why Boaz cautions Ruth against falling to the temptation to seek other opportunities.[49] Second, he provides the alternative: "Stay here with [literally, 'cling on to'] the women who work for me. . . . and follow along after the women" (2:8–9). This dual instruction indicates that whether or not the overseer has given Ruth permission to glean among the sheaves, now Boaz expressly allows it. What is more, Boaz tells Ruth that he has ordered his male servants (literally, "young men") "not to lay a hand on you" (literally, "not to touch you"). While some scholars understand this phrase "not to touch you" as an instruction to not bother Ruth in her work,[50] several scholars agree that this explicitly forbids sexual harassment.[51] Harvesttime was well-known for this,[52] and Boaz shows concern for Ruth's safety.

Thus, with his opening words, Boaz fulfills his obligations to a needy clanswoman. His words are set into a concentric structure of repeating key vocabulary (2:8–9):[53]

Rhetorical question	Listen to me (literally, "have you not heard . . . ?")	
Instruction 1	Don't go (*halak*)	and glean in another (*aher*) field
Instruction 2	Follow along (*halak*)	after (*aḥʿrê*) the women
Rhetorical question	I have told the men not to lay a hand on you (literally, "Have I not commanded . . . ?")	

Finally, Boaz authorizes Ruth to "drink from the water jars the men have filled." This gesture, as scholars observe, goes beyond providing for Ruth's physical needs. In a culture where foreigners draw and carry water for the Israelites (Josh 9:27), and women for men (Gen 24:10–20), and where Moabites are particularly denounced for their historic lack of hospitality towards Israel

---

49. Neusner, *Ruth Rabbah*, XXXV:i.2.
50. Pressler, *Joshua, Judges and Ruth*, 279.
51. Block, *Judges, Ruth*, 659–660.
52. Thus, the possible grape-gathering ditty in Song of Songs 2:15: "Catch for us the foxes, the little foxes that ruin the vineyards, our vineyards that are in bloom." The vineyards are the young women, and the foxes the young men who make (often unwelcome) advances on them.
53. See Linafelt, *Ruth*, 33.

(Deut 23:3–4), Boaz's allows Ruth the Moabite woman to drink water from the jars that Israelite men have filled. An Indian equivalent would be to allow a lower-caste woman to drink from the same well or vessel that a higher-caste person uses – unthinkable in most parts of the country. For Ruth, this is extraordinary care,[54] verging on exceptional privilege if not an outright honor.

So overcome is Ruth at this unexpected kindness that she "bowed down with her face to the ground." Besides being used before deity,[55] this gesture was common as an expression of gratitude or homage between humans (e.g., Gen 23:7; 33:3; 2 Kgs 2:15).[56] An equivalent in Indian culture is the *charan sparsh* ("to touch [another's] feet"), a common demonstration of respect towards anyone considered superior such as elders, parents, or teachers.

Bowing down to the ground, Ruth asks Boaz the question that baffles her: "Why have I found such favor in your eyes that you notice me – a foreigner?" This is a rhetorical question, for it "bespeaks her humble gratitude."[57] What is more, Ruth's acknowledgment of finding favor takes us back to the wish with which she started the day – she hoped to find someone who would favor her with permission to glean on his field (2:2). The storyteller is letting us know that now her hope has been fulfilled, not in the young overseer but in Boaz. Ruth's finding favor takes us back even further in the story, to the day she left Moab with Naomi. On that day, Naomi had attempted to bid Ruth farewell with the blessing that Ruth would "find [vb. *matza*] rest in the home of another husband" (1:9). This day, Ruth finds not rest (vb. *matza*) but favor. That the words "rest" (*manuha*) and "favor" (*hen*) share the same consonants could suggest that once "favor" has been found, "rest" might well follow.[58]

Boaz has "noticed" (vb. *nkr*) Ruth. Here, "noticing" means "to pay attention to." Ruth considers herself an unlikely candidate to receive such attention since she is a foreigner (the noun *nokriya*, meaning foreigner, is homonymous with the verb *nkr*). The sentence plays with similar sounding words which, in English, could be rendered: "You are giving recognition to someone who cannot be recognized as your own." At this point, we, who know that Boaz is Ruth's clansman, cannot help wondering if Ruth's gratitude is excessive. As

54. Younger, *Judges and Ruth*, 444.
55. Pressler, *Joshua, Judges and Ruth*, 280. For example, Numbers 20:6; Judges 13:20; 1 Kings 18:39.
56. Bush, *Ruth-Esther*, 122; Younger, *Judges and Ruth*, 444–445.
57. Pressler, *Joshua, Judges and Ruth*, 280.
58. Significantly, and relevant to this context, the Hebrew word *hen* ("favor") is often used in reference to sexual desirability (Nah 3:4; Prov 11:16; 31:30; Esth 2:15, 17), and the inability of a wife to find *hen* in the eyes of her husband could be a reason for divorce (Deut 24:1).

kinsman, is not Boaz obliged to take care of Ruth?[59] But we must remember two things. First, in the period of the judges, the law had fallen by the wayside and "everyone did as they saw fit" (Judg 21:25). Second, even though Boaz is a kinsman, there is one other whose obligation to care for Naomi's family supersedes his (3:12). Yet Boaz states his responsibility to Ruth in a well-informed and spirited response (2:11–12).

Boaz recounts what he has heard about Ruth. Her noble actions outweigh the humble state to which her current socioeconomic position as a destitute foreigner confines her. When he says that he has "been told all about what you have done for your mother-in-law since the death of your husband," he is referring to Ruth's "kindness" (*hesed*) towards her mother-in law in leaving (*azav*) her parents and her homeland in order to "come to live with a people you did not know before." This shows that Boaz had learned about Ruth's commitment to her mother-in-law (1:16–17); this commitment, as we have already noted, parallels and, arguably, even exceeds Abraham's commitment in leaving all to obey God (compare Gen 12:1; 24:7),[60] since Ruth neither experienced a specific call nor was promised any blessing.[61] In contrast to our times, people of the ancient world viewed having to leave home calamitous rather than as an opportunity to seek fortune elsewhere.[62] Ruth's "kindness" (*hesed*) has earned her this extravagant "favor" (*hen*). Her willingness to abandon (*azav*) her people in favor of clinging (*davaq* 1:14) to an Israelite mother-in-law has been rewarded with the invitation to stay (literally, "cling to"; *davaq*) with Boaz's harvesters (2:8). Ruth has found another community. Her integration into Israelite society has begun.

In appreciation of her kindness to his kinswoman Naomi, Boaz concludes by invoking the Lord on behalf of Ruth. Translated, keeping the Hebrew word order for the first line (2:12), the blessing goes:

> The LORD repays (vb. *shlm*) your work and may it be a rich (adj. *shelemah*) reward (*maskoret*) from the LORD, the God of Israel, under whose wings (pl. of *kanaf*) you have come to take refuge.

We notice that the object of the first line is Ruth – her work and its well-deserved reward. Significantly, this is bracketed by the Lord. He is the subject, the one who acts to reward. Even though these are Boaz's words, this is clearly

---

59. Linafelt, *Ruth*, 38.
60. Gow, *The Book of Ruth*, 54.
61. Davis and Parker, *Who Are You, My Daughter?*, 49.
62. Davis and Parker, 49.

the narrator's theme for the book itself – the honor God bestows on the Moabite Ruth.

There are several words here that catch the reader's attention. First, there is the noun "reward." Boaz seems to be acknowledging that what he has done for Ruth is not a sufficient recompense.[63] An apt repayment would be that she be "richly rewarded" by the Lord, the God of Israel. This word "reward" (n. fem. *maskoret*) brings back yet another echo of equivalence between Ruth and Abraham, for it is also God's promise to Abram: "I am your shield, your very great reward (n. masc. *sakar*)" (Gen 15:1). What is more, this promise of a great reward to Abram is closely connected with God's promise of progeny to Abram.[64] The ancient reader must have heard the resonance with the patriarchal story and perhaps also with Psalm 127:3, where offspring are a reward (*sakar*).[65] Boaz's use of the word is pregnant with unintended meaning.

Second, there is the word "wings." Boaz justifies his invocation of divine compensation by pointing out that Ruth has taken refuge under the Lord's wings (pl. of the sg. *kanaf*; see 3:9). Here Boaz echoes an image found elsewhere in the OT of the Lord as a mother bird that spreads its wings over its young ones as they come scurrying to her for protection from danger (Pss 36:7 [Hebrew 36:8]; 91:4).[66] Boaz is interpreting Ruth's choice as being not simply in favor of Naomi but in favor of the Lord himself.[67] There is an element of irony in Boaz's words. At the end of the harvest season, Ruth is going to ask Boaz to marry her. Using an idiomatic expression, she will request that he spread the corner of his garment (*kanaf*) over her (3:9). Eventually, it will be Boaz who becomes the progeny-providing agent. Of course, at this point, Boaz is unaware that he speaks a prophecy that he himself will fulfil.

Third, there is the root *shlm*, used twice, both times to describe what Ruth should receive from the Lord: he should recompense her (vb. *shlm*) with a full (adj. *shelemah*) wage. Considering the immediate association the context has with *shalom* (fullness, well-being), we recall the last time Ruth received a blessing (from Naomi) and the parallels between the two:

1:9	2:12
May the LORD	May the LORD . . . by the LORD

63. Hubbard, *The Book of Ruth*, 165.
64. Nielsen, *Ruth*, 59.
65. Gow, *The Book of Ruth*, 55.
66. Davis and Parker, *Who Are You, My Daughter?*, 51.
67. Block, *Judges, Ruth*, 663–664.

grant	repay
rest	richly rewarded
in the home of [another] husband	under [his] wings

The divine name is doubled, and the other elements are intensified. Thus the Lord will not merely be a benefactor who grants but a debtor who settles what is due. Instead of merely the rest (or, security) Naomi had hoped for Ruth, Boaz wishes Ruth *shalom*, a completeness that includes security and goes beyond security. This security, Naomi thinks, will come through marriage. Boaz asks that it come from being under the Lord's protection; but, as we will see, the agency of that social protection will be marriage to Boaz.

Of course, while the readers relish this dexterous layering of the future and the present, much of it escapes the characters engaged in the dialogue. Ruth's response to Boaz demonstrates that she has clearly paid attention to the favorable relationship that is developing between herself and Boaz. Nevertheless, she does not take advantage of it. Addressing Boaz deferentially as "my lord" (*adoni*; an equivalent of "sir"), she voices the hope that she may continue to find favor in his eyes. We will note here that *adon* can be used for God as well as for a human superior – a point we will return to.

"You have put me at ease by speaking kindly," Ruth says. The expression "put me at ease" is literally "comforted me," and the expression "speaking kindly" is literally "speaking to the heart." While these two expressions can legitimately indicate speaking words of encouragement and comfort, Pressler notes that when a man directs such speech to a woman, it can indicate that he is wooing her.[68] In Ruth's innocent expressions of gratitude is yet another proleptic reference to the happy turns of plot that await the speakers. The nuanced dialogue adds to the stage already set for a productive romance, an appealing sensory cluster of sight, smell, and sound: the expanse of golden fields, the scent of grain freshly harvested, and harvesttime ditties that fall pleasantly on the ear.[69] At this point, however, Ruth sees herself as socially not even equivalent to Boaz's "servant" (*shifhah*), a term generally used to refer to a female slave on the lowest rung of society.[70] Ruth's self-evaluation as less than a servant (*shifhah*) arises from her identity as a Moabite foreigner (*nokriya*). She sees herself as an outsider to the Bethlehemite community. Before the day is done, she will have information that changes her outsider status.

---

68. Pressler, *Joshua, Judges and Ruth*, 281.
69. See Hubbard, *The Book of Ruth*, 135.
70. Younger, *Judges and Ruth*, 445–446.

2:14 Boaz's Second Act of Kindness

The day wears on, and when it is time for the midday meal Boaz performs his second act of kindness. If his first act was reported solely as dialogue, his second includes action. It starts with Boaz inviting Ruth to join his workers for lunch – "Come over here" – and by specifically including her in it: "Have some bread and dip it in the wine vinegar" (2:14). Boaz takes his kindness to Ruth a step further, enabling the "foreigner" to join the circle of Israelites. In addition, Boaz "offered her some roasted grain," more than enough to satisfy Ruth's need, such that she even had some grain left over after "she ate all she wanted."

This generous invitation to a meal might remind us of the generous meal that Christ served to the crowds that followed him (Matt 14:13–21; Mark 6:30–44; Luke 9:10–17; John 6:1–15). There, similarly, "all ate and were satisfied . . . [and had] twelve basketfuls of broken pieces that were left over" (Matt 14:20, compare John 6:12–13). Boaz is often viewed as prefiguring Christ. As the antitype to Boaz, Christ exceeds Boaz. Not only does he provide his people bread for the day, he pronounces himself the bread which gives life eternal (John 6:51–58).

2:15–17 Boaz's Third Act of Kindness

Ruth finds that good fortune, like troubles, also comes in threes! Boaz performs a third act of kindness.

After the meal, as Ruth got up to glean, he ordered his men to "let her gather among the sheaves" without reprimand. Scholars have often found this order difficult to reconcile with 2:7, in which Ruth seeks permission to glean among the sheaves. Therefore, some suggest that the permission Ruth earlier sought from the overseer is granted to her only now in 2:15 by the landowner himself.[71] However, as already noted in the comment on 2:7, we assume that the overseer had granted the permission to Ruth. So we wonder why Boaz sees the need to reissue that permission. We find out in the next verse.

Reading the next verse, we understand that Boaz reissues the permission so that he can add a further privilege: "Even pull out some stalks for her from the bundles and leave them for her to pick" (2:16). By reserving for Boaz the words of permission to glean among the sheaves, the narrator does two things: First, the act of kindness is credited to Boaz rather than shared with

---

71. Pressler, *Joshua, Judges and Ruth*, 279.

the overseer, even though the overseer earlier allowed Ruth a special privilege;[72] and second, pronouncing the permission gives Boaz the opportunity to add on the extraordinary allowance of crops intentionally left behind for Ruth to glean. Ruth is elevated from being a gleaner who gathers a subsistence living to a gleaner who not only gathers among the sheaves but for whose sake heads of grain from the bundles are intentionally pulled out.

Boaz's instructions to his workers have a synonymously parallel structure:[73]

| 2:15 | Let her gather among the sheaves | and don't reprimand her |
| 2:16 | Even pull out some stalks for her from the bundles and leave them for her to pick up | and don't rebuke her |

Precisely because of the extraordinary nature of the two instructions, Boaz needs to add the riders that will protect Ruth from disgruntled laborers who see no reason why she should receive such high privileges. In later centuries, the rabbis took Boaz's order to mean that the giver should ensure that the needy should never feel humiliated in receiving. So they would drop coins or lentils, as if unintentionally, for their poorer colleagues to pick up later.[74]

All this in no way diminishes Ruth's diligence at work. She literally "makes hay while the sun shines" ("from morning"; 2:7, "until evening"; 2:17). As her work hours ended, Ruth threshed the barley she had gathered. The Hebrew verb used here for threshing refers not to the large-scale threshing done at a threshing floor but to a small-scale threshing of grain done by beating the stalks and the ears with a stick.[75] This separates out the chaff from the grain, reducing the weight of the harvested material to a minimum.

Surprisingly, even this minimized weight amounted to an *ephah*. There is no consensus among scholars on the modern equivalent of an *ephah*, not even on whether it is a measure of volume or weight. For example, while Bush suggests that this measure could translate as something between 22 liters and 36.4 liters in volume,[76] Nielsen thinks that an *ephah* would equal anything between 29 US pounds (approximately 13 kilograms) and 50 US pounds

72. Block, *Judges, Ruth*, 668.
73. Synonymous parallelism is a poetic device where the statement in the first line is repeated in the second line, with key words of the first line being replaced by their synonyms in the second line. For example, in Proverbs 3:11 (italics added): "My son, do not *despise* the LORD's *discipline*, and do not *resent* his *rebuke*."
74. Neusner, *Ruth Rabbah*, XLII:i.1
75. Bush, *Ruth-Esther*, 132.
76. Bush, 133.

(approximately 22.5 kilograms) in weight.[77] Whichever the exact equivalence, we see that Ruth has gleaned a very large quantity of grain in just one day. This quantity becomes striking considering the fact that the average ration of a laborer in ancient West Asia (particularly in ancient Babylonia) was between half a kilogram to one kilogram of grain per day.[78] At the end of the day, Ruth leaves the field with exorbitantly more than Boaz's workmen did! We now understand why Boaz had to command his harvesters not to ill-treat Ruth (2:9, 15, 16).

2:18–22 BACK AT HOME

From public space, the scene shifts back to the privacy of a home. Ruth has returned bearing the profit of her day's work.

The sight of the enormous quantity of grain takes Naomi by surprise. But that is not all that Ruth has brought home: "Ruth also brought out and gave her what she had left over after she had eaten enough" (2:18). As Hubbard puts it, that Ruth brought back such a quantity of grain was reason for astonishment. But that she also returns with cooked food beggars belief.[79] These carefully saved leftovers from lunch become an expression of "kindness" through a dual agency. This food was served by Boaz's generous hands to Ruth, whose hands in turn brought them to Naomi. We can't help hoping that now at least Naomi is beginning to see that she was exaggerating her plight – by completely leaving Ruth out of the equation – with her assertion that she has returned from Moab "empty" (1:21). Naomi's aged hands are surely trembling with happy anticipation of news as they are filled with the unexpected food.

Indeed, her words tumble out in the form of two questions[80] (both asking essentially the same thing), followed by a blessing on the unknown benefactor, for Naomi knew full well that such weighty returns could not have been gained without the cooperation of some landowner. Naomi exclaims: "Where did you glean today? Where did you work? Blessed be the man who took notice of you!" (2:19). Her first word, ironically, is *ephoh* ("where?"), an interrogative that sounds very similar to the quantity of grain Ruth is carrying into the house – an *ephah* (2:17). In a chapter that is dense with multi-layered phrases, this play on words is delightful in its simplicity. What is more, we know more than

---

77. Nielsen, *Ruth*, 61.
78. Pressler, *Joshua, Judges and Ruth*, 281; Bush, *Ruth-Esther*, 133.
79. Hubbard, *The Book of Ruth*, 181.
80. Hubbard, 183.

either Ruth or Naomi know at this point, so the conversation that follows is entertaining simply because we want to see the look on Naomi's face, and then on Ruth's, as they fill in each other's ignorance. It takes a skillful storyteller to keep an audience hooked by using predictability rather than suspense!

Ruth answers Naomi's questions with a construction that closely parallels the introduction of Boaz in 2:1. She describes the man in a long sentence that ends with his name. We turn to see what effect this has on Naomi.

Upon hearing the name of the benefactor, Naomi spontaneously responds with another blessing. Her first one had been generic: "Blessed be the man . . . !" (2:19). Now she exclaims: "The LORD bless him! . . . He has not stopped showing his kindness to the living and the dead" (2:20).

How should we read this? One way is to interpret "The LORD bless him!" as Naomi's benediction on Boaz. The Lord would bless Boaz because he – *the Lord* – continues to show kindness to the living (Boaz) as he did to the dead (Naomi's deceased family members).[81] Another way is to read "The LORD bless him!" as a commendation of Boaz to the Lord for the reason that he – *Boaz* – has not stopped showing his kindness to the living (Ruth and Naomi) and, through them, to the dead (his deceased kinsmen).[82] This ambiguity concerning the object of Naomi's blessing – Is it the Lord? Is it Boaz? – cunningly interweaves divine initiative with human agency.

The expression "the living and the dead" is a merism,[83] and so includes Naomi's entire family. With this begins a reversal of Naomi's outlook. Finally, we have evidence that she sees that she has no reason to consider herself afflicted by God (compare 1:20–21). On the contrary, she is the recipient of kindness beyond expectation.

Now it is Naomi's turn to surprise Ruth, and at her words, we turn to watch for Ruth's expression. Naomi says: "That man is our close relative [*qarob*]; he is one of our guardian-redeemers [*goel*]" (2:20). Naomi includes Ruth in the family circle, referring to Boaz as "our" relative. This is a reversal for one who had, not so long ago, asked Ruth to return to her people (1:15).[84] The first term, *qarob,* is within the wider circle of relationships. It could even mean "friend" (Lev 25:25; Ps 15:3), though more often, it would mean "relative."

---

81. Refer to the Hebrew text of 2 Samuel 2:5, where David blesses the men of Jabesh Gilead in the name of the Lord for their kindness in bringing back Saul's body from the enemy's territory in words very similar to the blessing Naomi pronounces here.
82. See, Block, *Judges, Ruth*, 671–673.
83. *Merism* is a literary device where two opposite extremes are mentioned, in order to refer to everything in between. For example, "*head* to *toe*" or "*heaven* and *earth*" (Gen 1:1).
84. Davis and Parker, *Who Are You, My Daughter?*, 61.

Goel is more specific. In ancient Israel, a "redeemer" was a male benefactor of the family, who would be responsible for the welfare of the family.[85] As Block observes, the role of this redeemer would play out in at least five different ways, as set out in different OT passages:

> (1) to ensure that the hereditary property of the clan never passes out of its possession by buying back the ancestral land that a poor relative might have sold (Lev 25:25–30); (2) to maintain the freedom of individuals within the clan by buying back those who have sold themselves into slavery because of poverty (Lev 25:47–55); (3) to track down and execute murderers of near relatives (Num 35:12, 19–27); (4) to receive restitution money on behalf of a deceased victim of a crime (Num 5:8); and (5) to ensure that justice is served in a lawsuit involving a relative (Job 19:25; Ps 119:154; Jer 50:34).[86]

In general, a redeemer would demonstrate corporate solidarity that would ensure the welfare of the family and the clan. In the welfare of the family lies the welfare of the individual, and in the welfare of the individual rests the welfare of the family. Rudyard Kipling's poem, used in the movie *The Jungle Book* (which is set in India), expresses it well: "As the creeper that girdles the tree trunk / the law runneth forward and back; / For the strength of the pack is the wolf / and the strength of the wolf is the pack."[87] Hence, by calling Boaz "one of our guardian-redeemers," Naomi appears to hope that his goodwill towards her – as evidenced by his actions so far – will lead to further happy developments. We cannot be sure this will happen, though. After all, Boaz is only "one of" the several guardian-redeemers (sometimes referred to as kinsman-redeemers) with obligations to Elimelek's family.

Ruth the Moabite, perhaps being a stranger to the system of "guardian-redeemer," does not seem to get the weight of Naomi's excitement about Boaz being one of their guardian-redeemers.[88] Or perhaps she is still overwhelmed by the enormity of the kindness shown to her by Boaz. Either way, she prattles on excitedly, recounting how Boaz has invited her to glean right up to when he finishes harvesting. Having seen his fields, Ruth is perhaps aware that Boaz

85. Pressler, *Joshua, Judges and Ruth*, 282.
86. Block, *Judges, Ruth*, 147.
87. Rudyard Kipling, "The Law of the Jungle," http://www.kiplingsociety.co.uk/poems_lawofjungle.htm.
88. Block, *Judges, Ruth*, 676.

grows two crops. Once the current barley season is over, the wheat season will commence.

In the middle of all the excitement, Naomi wisely slips in a word of caution. Ruth has reported that Boaz has asked Ruth to "stay with [his] workers" (masc. pl.). Naomi is old enough to know that this has its risks. She echoes Boaz's advice from earlier in the day (2:8–9), advising Ruth to stay with the women workers, and to refrain from venturing into any other fields, lest harm should befall her. If Boaz had used the euphemism "lay a hand on you," Naomi uses a more explicit Hebrew word – "harmed" here could mean attack or molestation.[89] These acts of violence against socially disadvantaged groups would have been far from uncommon "in the days when the judges ruled" (1:1; compare Judg 17:6; 21:25). What is more, Ruth would have been easy prey on two accounts: First, the law had no regulation for intercourse with a widow; and second, since she was "a foreigner from a disliked ethnic group,"[90] Israelite males could well have raped her in the name of national sentiment.[91] In today's India, where women, and even girl children, of religious minorities are similarly at risk, we respect Ruth all the more for her courage and appreciate Naomi for her wisdom and motherly concern.

2:23 CLOSING NOTE

The closing note tells us that Ruth took Naomi's advice to heart. She restricted her work to Boaz's field for the duration of the two harvests, and wisely kept herself in the company of the women workers. This would cover a period of about seven weeks, concluding with Pentecost (compare Deut 16:9–12), ranging roughly from late April to early June.[92]

This length of time, we might think, would present a slew of opportunities for the relationship between Boaz and Ruth to develop into romance.[93] But, to our disappointment, nothing eventful happens. The harvest season ends. There will be no further occasion for their paths to cross. Naomi and Ruth have enough to subsist on for now, but the end of the harvest signals the end of further provision.[94] The immediate problem is solved, but the future is as bleak as when the chapter began.

89. Bush, *Ruth-Esther*, 139–140.
90. Sakenfeld, *Ruth*, 43.
91. LaCocque, *Ruth*, 79–80.
92. Bush, *Ruth-Esther*, 140.
93. Younger, *Judges and Ruth*, 450.
94. LaCocque, *Ruth*, 80.

Bracketing this very eventful day are notes announcing the beginning and end of the harvest season (1:22 and 2:23).[95] This indication of plenty only throws into relief the fact that the two widows continue in uncertainty over provision for their future.

CONCLUSION

The observant reader will notice that though the chapter begins and closes with a family of two widows, there are clues that there may be changes ahead. One clue is in how Ruth's status has changed over the course of the day's event. She was introduced as a Moabite (2:2); on receiving a welcome not usually accorded to a Moabite, she referred to herself as "a foreigner" (2:10); with Boaz's kind words, she feels sufficiently integrated into the Bethlehemite group to call herself his "servant" (*shifhah*; 2:13); and by the end of the day, she learns that Boaz is not just a benefactor but bonded to her as guardian-redeemer – very much a prospect for marriage (2:20). So even though the chapter concludes with Ruth still a Moabite (2:21), who can tell where Ruth will wind up when the story ends!

The second clue is the anticipation that if Ruth has been so phenomenally fruitful in the field, she will be as much or more so in the home. Grain in her arms promises seed in her womb. This leads us to the third clue, which the narrator has cleverly embedded into their conversation. As we noted, Boaz blessed Ruth with the protection of Yahweh's "wings" (*kanaf*), which is also how the business of marriage is described – a man extends his *kanaf* over the woman he marries. She replied requesting his continued "favor" (*hen*). From Naomi's lips, we heard the interlinking of Yahweh with Boaz – that "he" continues to show "kindness" (*hesed*). Thus, as Yahweh is to Naomi in restoring her fortunes, so Boaz will be to Ruth.

Of course, the characters themselves are unaware that their words are pregnant with future fulfilment. By overlapping God the divine benefactor with Boaz, his human agent, the wily narrator has set the stage for what happens in the next episode of the story.

---

95. LaCocque, 59.

HESED, READ ALONGSIDE THE HINDU VIRTUE OF *DAANA*[1]

Hindu folklore tells the story of king Rantideva, an exemplar of selfless charity. When his kingdom was laid waste by a famine, he undertook a fast of forty-eight days, refusing to break it till he was assured that his subjects had been cared for. But even as he broke his fast with a glass of water, he heard a cry of thirst, and promptly offered his drink to the needy man. As he sat down to eat, a hungry guest turned up at his door, and he gave his meal to him. Then, turning to his courtiers who were understandably anxious about his well-being, he explained that his good deeds were not motivated by personal gain – that is, the hope of achieving *moksha* ("salvation") by deliverance from rebirth into the physical world. Rather, his charity was for the sake of his people and substitutionary in some mystical sense: "I take on myself their suffering so that they may be rid of their misery."[2]

Daana ("giving") is considered a part of Hindu *dharma* (moral duty) and one of its highest virtues.[3] This duty begins within the extended family and reaches beyond it to the world at large. The householder is urged to care for the welfare of others even at his own expense, as in the story of Rantideva. The sacred text of Hinduism, *Bhagavad Gita*, endorses giving without any expectation of reward;[4] but the hope of personal advantage persists in popular thinking – for example, the belief that giving can neutralize the ill-effects of one's horoscope. Among the various forms of philanthropic giving, what is within the commoner's ability to do is *anna daana* ("the giving of food"). It is a meaningful act of charity, especially in a country marked by poverty, and in which drought-caused famine is hardly news. So family celebrations often include large-scale feeding of the poor. And perhaps even the state-sponsored schemes for midday meals at government-run schools, and heavily subsidized food in "Indira canteens" belong to this tradition of *anna daana*.

---

1. With inputs from Francis Mathew, "Exegesis of Ruth," MDiv Class, SAIACS (Bangalore, 2019).
2. *Srimad Bhagavatam*, 9.
3. See Sharada Sugirtharajah, "Traditions of Giving in Hinduism," *Alliance Magazine*, September 2001, https://www.alliancemagazine.org/feature/traditions–of–giving–in–hinduism/. She cites the *Rig Veda* 10.117.1–2, 6: "The gods have not ordained that humans die of hunger;/ even to the well-fed man death comes in many shapes./ The wealth of the generous man never wastes away,/ but the niggard has none to console him."
4. *Bhagavad Gita*, 17.20–22.

When Indian Christians come to chapter 2 of the book of Ruth, they might consider if something like the Hindu virtue of *daana* is in operation – especially since Boaz generously gives grain and food to Ruth, and Ruth equally generously saves and brings home some of this food to Naomi. The Hebrew words equivalent to *daana* ("giving") are *hen* and *hesed*. Let's take a quick look at these.

Hesed first finds a mention in Naomi's speech as she invokes blessings on her daughters-in-law, Orpah and Ruth (1:8). The word *hesed* sits at the heart of Naomi's benediction. She invokes divine *hesed* on her daughters-in-law so as to honor their *hesed* to their deceased husbands and Naomi.[5] Naomi hopes that this divine *hesed* will mediate remarriages for Orpah and Ruth (1:9a). We understand from this that human *hesed* can become "the measure" for divine *hesed*.[6]

In chapter 2, the words *hen* and *hesed* intertwine.[7] In the morning, Ruth leaves the house on her gleaning mission hoping to find *hen* ("favor") in someone's eyes (2:2). Before the morning has turned to midday, Ruth discovers – to her amazement – that she has found *hen* in the eyes of the wealthy Boaz (2:10, 13). At the end of the day, back at home, Naomi interprets this demonstration of *hen* as *hesed*. We have seen that Naomi's ambiguous turn of phrase allow for both Boaz and Yahweh to be the source of *hesed*. (See commentary on 2:20.)

If Naomi is referring to human *hesed*, then it refers to Boaz's generosity that exceeded the legal provisions of gleaning. But if Naomi is referring to God as the antecedent, then she perceives divine *hesed* as being experienced through human actions.[8] We understand from this that divine *hesed* is channeled into the world through human agency.

The third and final mention of *hesed* occurs in 3:10. Boaz extols Ruth's two distinct acts of *hesed*. While the first act of *hesed* – Ruth's loyalty and service to Naomi – was praiseworthy, her second act of *hesed* – choosing to marry Boaz – is even more so, he says.[9] Ruth, being free of any legal obligation, could have married somebody else (3:10b). But she chooses to marry Naomi's aged relative knowing that this will accomplish two ends: (i) Naomi's security and (ii) the perpetuation of Elimelek's line, through the system of levirate marriage.[10] We understand

5. Nielsen, *Ruth*, 46.
6. Linafelt, *Ruth*, 11.
7. Selson Bensly, "Exegesis of Ruth," MDiv Class, SAIACS (Bangalore, 2019).
8. Sakenfeld, *Ruth*, 48.
9. Nielsen, *Ruth*, 76.
10. Sakenfeld, *Ruth*, 61–62.

from this that *hesed* exceeds *hen*. While *hen* may be generosity that flows out of one's abundance, *hesed* may entail cost to oneself.

Let us see how *hesed* compares with the Hindu virtue of *daana* ("giving"). First, the measure of giving: *daana* may be similar to *hen*, in which case one gives out of a fatly bulging pocket. Or, *daana* may be similar to *hesed*, as in Rantideva's case, where one gives sacrificially.

Second, the object of the giving: Rantideva gives to his own people. So do most Hindus. *Hesed,* while often directed at the community of faith, also crosses borders. King David promises *hesed* towards Hanun, an Ammonite king, in response to similar kindness shown him by Hanun's recently deceased father Nahash (2 Sam 10:2; 1 Chr 19:2). Rahab pleads for and receives *hesed* at the hands of the Israelites invading Canaan (Josh 2:12, 14). As for divine *hesed*, the prophet Jonah is proved right that Yahweh will extend his *hesed* even beyond Israel's borders, to Nineveh (Jonah 4:2).

Third, the motivation for giving: Rantideva's rationale – that is, to absorb vicariously the suffering of the starving – has no parallel biblical idea within human-human demonstrations of *hesed*. But setting Rantideva aside, we find that the Hindu on the street does *daana* not for vicarious reasons but for personal gain. They believe that giving may avert misfortunes lurking in their horoscope and waiting to strike or that it may store up *punya* (merit) for their next birth. Perhaps this parallels the idea in Ruth that human *hesed* prompts divine *hesed*. Both Naomi and Boaz speak as if Ruth's *hesed* should (and will) prompt Yahweh's *hesed* – supplying her immediate need of food, and eventually supplying her long-term need of family. Indeed, a little like the typical Hindu, we are confident that our acts of philanthropy will be rewarded either in this life or in the afterlife (e.g., Luke 6:38; Rev 22:12). There are, however, far greater motivations for *hesed*.

One higher motivation for practicing *hesed* is to give so as to set a good example. Gleaning, for example, was mandated by law. While on one hand the motivation for allowing gleaning on your fields was so that God would bless the work of your hands (Deut 24:19), the other purpose was that the gleaning laws would form a habit of doing for others what others had not done for them: "Remember that you were slaves in Egypt. That is why I command you to do this" (Deut 24:22). This chapter in Ruth portrays giving as a communal obligation – not a voluntary act deserving admiration, as Rantideva's did.

A second, higher, motivation is the one fundamental to the practice of *hesed*: *hesed* conforms our nature to the nature of God. *Hesed* is a distinctive of Yahweh (Exod 34:6). Similarly, the adjective *hanun* ("gracious"), related to the noun *hen* ("favor"), is another descriptor of Yahweh (e.g., Exod 34:6). Israel was required to be like Yahweh (Lev 19:2), and practicing *hesed* was to mirror him. This is also Paul's argument when he urges the Corinthian church to "excel in the grace of giving . . . For you know the grace of our Lord Jesus Christ, that though he was rich, yet for your sake he became poor, so that you through his poverty might become rich" (2 Cor 8:7, 9).

How, then, might we define *hesed*, a concept unique to Christian faith and practice? It has been translated variously as "covenant loyalty, faithfulness, kindness, goodness, mercy, love, and compassion,"[11] but it might need more than a word to extract its full essence: It is an unswerving commitment to the good of another, even at cost to oneself, motivated by, and modeled on, Jesus.

Havilah Dharamraj

---

11. Younger, *Judges and Ruth*, 393.

RUTH 3

A man was passing through a forest one day and came upon a tiger trapped in a cage. The tiger pleaded to be let out. Naturally, the man firmly refused. "Of course, I won't! You'll pounce on me and eat me!" The tiger continued to beg. "I will be so grateful that I will be your slave for life," it promised. The man relented and let the tiger out. The tiger promptly sprang upon the man. "What's to prevent me eating you now!" the tiger sneered. "You're a fool for thinking I would behave differently."

The man pleaded for his life, and the tiger agreed that he could present his case before a third party. A fox came by, and the man asked him to adjudicate. The fox asked for the details. On being told them, he looked baffled. "You were in the cage and the tiger was passing by?" he asked. "No, no!" growled the tiger, impatient to get on with his meal. "I was in the cage and the man came by." "I'm not sure," said the fox, scratching his head in puzzlement. "Perhaps the cage was in you, and the man was passing by?" After a few rounds of this, the tiger jumped into the cage. "I was in the cage," he roared, "like this!" "Ah, I see now," said the cunning fox, and slammed the door shut on the tiger. Never trust a tiger.

The central episode of Ruth chapter 3 is something like this. Ruth, like the tiger, has a certain reputation. The readers expect that she will conduct herself like the Moabite she is, one descended from a daughter of Lot, who would not stop at incest to get what she wanted (Gen 19). The story now gives this less-than-reputable identity close attention. The harvest season provided Ruth a passage into the small farming community in the town of Bethlehem; but when chapter 2 ends, she remains as much a Moabite as when the chapter began (2:2, 21). When the story picks up after a couple of months, Ruth is going to have every opportunity to reprise her female forebears. The narrator, however, will invite us to compare the story with that of a bizarre intrafamilial sexual liaison perpetrated by another non-Israelite – the Canaanite Tamar (Gen 38). By the time we are done with setting Ruth's story alongside those of Lot's daughters and Tamar, we will find that we've peeled off, bit by scaly bit, the undesirable Moabite gray that coated Ruth's reputation.[1] Indeed, "it

---

1. For parallels between Tamar and Ruth, see LaCocque, *Ruth*, 51.

is as if the loss of her identity as a Moabite is a prerequisite for becoming part of Israel's history."[2]

STRUCTURE

In structure, chapter 3 parallels chapter 2. There is a movement from private to public space and back again. Naomi and Ruth converse at home before and after Ruth heads out to a communal threshing floor to encounter Boaz.

	In the fields	At the threshing floor
a. Exchange between Naomi and Ruth	2:1–2	3:1–5
b. Ruth goes out and meets Boaz	2:3	3:6–7
c. Boaz inquires as to Ruth's identity	2:4–7	3:8–9
d. Boaz asks Ruth to stay; deems her worthy, gives her food and protection	2:8–17	3:10–15
e. Ruth reports back to Naomi and receives counsel	2:18–23	3:16–18

The characters that drive the plot, however, are reversed. While it was Ruth who initiated the events of chapter 2, it is Naomi who sets the ball rolling in chapter 3. The two widows seem to outdo each other in resourcefulness, giving us an extraordinary story that only allows men to take frontstage in the last quarter. While it was Boaz who started the conversation with Ruth in the fields, now it is Ruth who unexpectedly opens the exchange at the threshing floor. If Ruth was taken by surprise at Boaz's kindness (2:10), here Boaz will be taken aback at what he perceives as Ruth's kindness to him (3:10).

Trible summarizes the differences succinctly, showing that the two meetings are a study in contrasts: "The first meeting was by chance; the second is by choice. The first was in the fields; the second at the threshing floor. The first was public; the second private. The first was work; the second play. The

---

2. Ellen van Wolde, "Intertextuality: Ruth in Dialogue with Tamar," in *A Feminist Companion to Reading the Bible: Approaches, Methods and Strategies*, eds. Athalya Brenner and Carole Fontaine (Sheffield: Sheffield Academic, 1997), 426–451. The article explores the resonance between the Ruth and Tamar stories using the method of reception-centered intertextuality.

first was by day; the second by night. Yet both of them hold the potential for life and death."[3]

We will study this chapter under three major sections, based on the location of each scene: At home (vv. 1–5); at the threshing floor (vv. 6–15); back at home (vv. 16–18).

3:1–5 AT HOME

In Hebrew, this section is composed entirely of direct speech, except for six words (four at the beginning of 3:1, and two at the beginning of 3:5). As with the story so far, dialogue is the window the narrator provides for readers to get a good look at the protagonists.

Naomi, as Block explains at length, sets out the problem that is to be resolved.[4] It is the same one she had mentioned several months before, when she and her daughters-in-law were on the road to Bethlehem – the problem of widowhood. Ruth must be found a place of "rest" (1:9; 3:1). As we would say in India, this marriageable woman needs to be "settled" into a husband's home. In the OT, the idiom "to find a home/to find rest" is associated with several desirable benefits: bridal happiness (Jer 7:23), security (Jer 42:6), long life (Gen 12:13; Deut 4:40; 5:16, 33), marital prosperity (Jer 40:9), and many children (Deut 6:3).[5]

Some suggest that Naomi is seeking to recompense Ruth's faithful labor to keep them fed and provisioned.[6] Others propose that Naomi is continuing her commitment to Ruth's well-being, perhaps even over her own interests since losing Ruth to marriage could leave her with no one to care for her.[7] She expressly desires Ruth's good in a home "where you will be well provided for" (3:1). A third possibility emerges once Naomi begins to set out her solution to the problem of Ruth's situation of widowhood: "Now Boaz, with whose women you have worked, is a relative of ours" (3:2). In naming Boaz "a relative of ours" as that solution, perhaps Naomi hopes to kill two birds with one stone – the problem of security for both Ruth and Naomi. Boaz has already shown himself to be sensitive to his obligations as Naomi's kinsman (2:11–16). Fourth, with the end of the harvest season, Naomi must feel the

---

3. Phyllis Trible, *God and the Rhetoric of Sexuality* (Philadelphia: Fortress, 1978), 183.
4. Block, *Ruth*, 165–172.
5. Hubbard, *The Book of Ruth*, 198.
6. For example, Hubbard, *The Book of Ruth*, 198.
7. For example, Block, *Judges, Ruth*, 681.

pinch of living hand-to-mouth from harvest to harvest. A guardian-redeemer would help restore the fortunes of her family by redeeming, on her behalf, land that her husband Elimelek must have sold. If the same kinsman could also marry Ruth, then there would be an heir to inherit this land and keep the family name alive. Indeed, without this heir, the legal prescription of Numbers 27:8–11 would take effect:

> If a man dies and leaves no son, give his inheritance to his daughter. If he has no daughter, give his inheritance to his brothers. If he has no brothers, give his inheritance to his father's brothers. If his father had no brothers, give his inheritance to the nearest relative in his clan, that he may possess it. This is to have the force of law for the Israelites. . .

The law allows for the inheritance to move in several directions when the head of the house dies. Notice, however, that the inheritance never passes on to the widow (see also commentary on 4:3–4 where Boaz says Naomi is "selling" Elimelek's land). This leaves Naomi in a desperate situation, with no land to till and grow her own food.

The usual preference among many Asians for boy children stems from a similar dual interest – to keep family property safe by perpetuating the family name by the male line. So perhaps Naomi's scheming is motivated by some measure of self-interest, which is not entirely a slur on her character considering that Israelite law made provision for unhappy circumstances such as hers.

We must take note, however, that Naomi does not refer to Boaz as a "guardian-redeemer" (goel). She knows very well that he is only one of several with that obligation to her deceased husband Elimelek (2:20). She may even know that there is another who has a closer kinship and, therefore, a higher responsibility (3:12). If her scheme makes Boaz its centerpiece, it is because of the seemingly chance acquaintance that has happily developed into nearly two months of daily contact. Perhaps Naomi hopes that Boaz will perform the task of guardian-redeemer (goel) through a levirate marriage (compare Deut 25:5–10) – in which the levir (Latin: brother-in-law) marries the widow of his deceased brother – and is underplaying that hope by using for him the generic "relative" (mod'a).[8] While this might be the reason Naomi refers to Boaz as merely a "relative," Glover wonders if there is a throwback here to the infamous story of Ruth's ancestresses. Perhaps Naomi hopes that Ruth, like the

---

8. Contra, e.g., Bush, *Ruth-Esther*, 148.

daughters of Lot, specializes in taking advantage of drunken elderly relatives in order to provide for her own security![9]

Proceeding from this kinship relationship with Boaz, Naomi spells out the details of her scheme to force Boaz's hand. Appealing to relatives for a leg up comes naturally in South Asia, where the term "brother" can be used to cover quite an array of persons related either by blood or by marriage. "Brothers" may be located on very different branches of a family tree but can still be leaned on (sometimes rather heavily!) to fulfill family obligations. Naomi plans to do exactly that. Although she has stayed at home, while Ruth is the one who has been out working, Naomi has been quietly gathering information. She knows that "tonight" Boaz "will be winnowing barley on the threshing floor" (3:2) – the last of the harvesting processes, and the last chance for Ruth to turn her acquaintance with Boaz into something more permanent.[10] For a small farming community, the one in a small town like Bethlehem, it would have been uneconomical for each family to have a threshing floor of its own. A common one would have served the need.

We pause to remind ourselves what winnowing was about in ancient Israel and where it was done. Much like in rural India, to winnow, the threshed grain is tossed up in the air using a winnowing fork. This causes the wind to carry away the lighter chaff while the heavier grain drops to the ground. Threshing floors were ideally on hilltops, where the wind flow was best and the rock surface allowed the falling grain to remain dirt free.[11]

Why was Boaz winnowing barley at the end of wheat harvest, and why was he winnowing at night? Perhaps farmers delayed the winnowing of barley till the wheat had been brought in because that freed them from the pressure of having to thresh the barley while the wheat harvest was on.[12] As for the time of winnowing, it is possible that the gusty afternoon sea breeze would have been too strong for the grain, while the gentler night wind was better suited for this agricultural activity.[13] Be that as it may, wily Naomi will take advantage of the darkness of night for the scheme she has in mind. Boaz, like his fellow farmers, would spend the night at the threshing floor to keep his grain safe from thieves and fire.

---

9. Neil Glover, "Your People, My People: An Exploration of Ethnicity in Ruth," *JSOT* 33, no. 3 (2009): 293–313, here, 304.
10. LaCocque, *Ruth*, 88.
11. Block, *Judges, Ruth*, 682.
12. Pressler, *Joshua, Judges and Ruth*, 286.
13. Bush, *Ruth-Esther*, 150.

The scheme is a daring one. Ruth is to prepare herself to meet Boaz by washing and perfuming herself and putting on her "best clothes." If Bush is correct in his observation that the Mediterranean people were not able to bathe regularly due to scarcity of water, and so used perfumed oil to control the body odor,[14] then bathing and putting on perfume would be reserved for very special occasions. This context is, perhaps, the reason the instruction on clothes is rendered "get dressed in your best clothes" (3:3). Elsewhere, the combination of these three actions is used for the dressing up of a bride (Ezek 16:8–12).[15] We recall a biblical parallel in the account of David concluding his period of mourning over the loss of his newborn son by washing, anointing with perfumed oil, and wearing his *simla* (2 Sam 12:20).[16] On the other hand, as Bush and Younger point out, the Hebrew word for "cloak/garment" (*simla*) is essentially a word for a common garment which extends from shoulders to feet. This is the garment which, for a poor man, would double up as a blanket at night (Exod 22:25–26).[17] Perhaps Naomi's instruction is much more culturally pointed than we imagine. She could be asking Ruth to lay off her widow's garb in favor of more regular clothing so as to indicate to Boaz her availability for marriage.[18] It is possible that widows wore some kind of garments that identified them as such; this is also indicated in the reference to Tamar's widow's garb in Genesis 38:14. This makes a lot of sense in South Asia, where widows are generally expected to wear white, a color considered inauspicious, or at least one that does not attract attention. Red, on the other hand, is a bride's color of choice.

Looking (and smelling!) her best, Ruth is to "go down to the threshing floor." Then the plot thickens. Ruth is to keep herself hidden till Boaz finishes his meal and settles down for the night, and then she is to steal up to him, pull up his covering, and lie at his "feet." What happens after this is up to Boaz: "He will tell you what to do" (3:4). The surreptitious nature of the mission is reflected in the fact that, both in Naomi's speech and in the narrator's words, Boaz's identity is masked.[19] Except for the two places where Naomi and the narrator need to identify Boaz by name (3:2, 7), every other place in this chapter where the Hebrew employs a noun to denote Boaz, he is referred to

14. Bush, 150.
15. Bush, 151.
16. Block, *Judges, Ruth*, 684. Contra Sakenfeld, *Ruth*, 54.
17. Bush, *Ruth-Esther*, 150–151; Younger, *Judges and Ruth*, 459.
18. Younger, *Judges and Ruth*, 459.
19. Hubbard, *The Book of Ruth*, 202.

as "the man" (3:3, 8, 16, 18).[20] Of course, since in the dark "all cats are gray," Ruth is to carefully eliminate the possibility of mistaken identity: "note the place where he is lying" (3:4).

The plot Naomi hatched could go wrong in many ways. First, it was outrageous. The threshing floor was men's territory (3:14). No self-respecting woman went down there unless she had business to ply. Prostitution at threshing floors found a mention in Israel's list of sins (Hos 9:1). In the Hebrew, Naomi's vocabulary heaps up *double entendres*. There are the verbs "to go," "to know" (as in "don't let him know"), "to uncover," and "to lie down," innocent in themselves but regularly used to describe intercourse.[21] There is "feet," which was a euphemism for the private parts (e.g., male in Exod 4:25; Judg 3:24; 1 Sam 24:3; and female in Deut 28:57; Ezek 16:25).[22] Thus, in Hebrew, urine is referred to as "the water of the feet" (2 Kgs 18:27; Isa 36:12). And the "feet" are as far up as Ruth is to roll up Boaz's blanket! It is hard to know whether Naomi intends the plain sense or a "pick up."

Second, just as much as Naomi's idea was outrageous, it was dangerous. Ruth could get noticed by other men, and without a kindly Boaz to preempt unwanted attention (2:9, 22), she could easily become a victim. The lawless period of the judges records one of the worst cases of gang rape (Judges 19).

Third, Naomi's scheme had a hole – a big one. Even if Ruth evaded detection and presented herself to Boaz, there was no way she could guarantee a marriage proposal. The outcome was entirely up to Boaz, who could even have taken advantage of this situation and got away with it.[23]

We could attempt a kinder reading of Naomi: it is possible that uncovering another person's feet was a customary way of requesting for marriage;[24] and that Naomi had sufficient proof of Boaz's reliability – his *hesed* towards her family (2:20) – in trusting Ruth to his care. Sakenfeld rightly asks what prevented Naomi from taking the proposal to her kinsman herself.[25] We may conjecture that in ancient eastern cultures, as in South Asia today, such negotiations were made by men. Naomi has none to speak for her. What is more, in a strongly patriarchal system, tricking the male was easier than persuading

20. Although the NIV uses the proper noun "Boaz" in verse 16, the Hebrew reads "the man."
21. Bush, *Ruth-Esther*, 155; Sakenfeld, *Ruth*, 54.
22. Hubbard, *The Book of Ruth*, 203. See Harry J. Harm, "The Function of Double Entendre in Ruth Three," *JOTT* 7, no. 1 (1995): 19–27.
23. Younger, *Judges and Ruth*, 460.
24. Younger, 459.
25. Sakenfeld, *Ruth*, 55.

him, and sometimes, sex was a key part of the trick.[26] In the stories of Lot's daughters and Judah's daughter-in-law Tamar, those women used their bodies to get what they wanted. While we may have to catch our breath a little at Naomi's audacious scheme, LaCocque reminds us that she is a gutsy woman. On the death of all the males in her family, hers was the risky decision to return to Bethlehem. To sit about hoping that a second round of good fortune will put Ruth into Boaz's path is not in Naomi's style of leadership. Here is a wager – taken at the risk of "double or nothing." If there is a trap being laid, it is likely to spring shut on her rather than on Boaz.[27]

Ruth, however, responds without objection: "I will do whatever you say" (3:5). For someone who had vigorously resisted Naomi's instructions that she should find herself a Moabite husband, her agreeing to proposition an Israelite man under dodgy circumstances comes as a surprise.[28] While Bush concedes that this could be a demonstration of "the radical extent of her commitment to and trust in Naomi,"[29] he also notes that instead of slavishly following Naomi's plan to the letter Ruth makes some wise changes[30] and goes beyond her brief. Older Indian Christian readers of this text would hardly notice this, finding it culturally convenient to stop at the report that Ruth "did everything her mother-in-law told her to do" (3:5). Where deference to older family members is given high social value, texts like these can become heavy yokes that we place either on others or on ourselves. We need to read on to see how exactly Ruth tweaked Naomi's less-than-sound scheme.

3:6–15 AT THE THRESHING FLOOR

Ruth has reached the communal threshing floor. That she has identified Boaz among the many men is signaled by the use of his name: "When Boaz had finished eating and drinking and was in good spirits, he went over to lie down at the far end of the grain pile" (3:7). We must remember that we are seeing him through Ruth's eyes as we crouch behind a grain pile with her in the dark, body tense with the anxiety of being discovered by some passerby.

---

26. Other than the daughters of Lot and Tamar, some examples of women tricksters are Rebekah, who deceives the elderly Isaac (Gen 27), and Rachel, who deceives her father Laban over the missing household gods (Gen 31:30–35).

27. LaCocque, *Ruth*, 82–83.

28. Sakenfeld, *Ruth*, 55.

29. Bush, *Ruth-Esther*, 157.

30. Bush, *Ruth-Esther*, 157.

Meanwhile, Boaz, from what she can see (and probably hear as well), has eaten heartily, washing down his meal with wine, and is in "good spirits." This does not necessarily mean a state of inebriation as in Lot's story (Gen 19). After all, threshing is a celebratory event, and Boaz's "heart is feeling good" (as the literal Hebrew reads). He is relaxed,[31] and "at peace with the world"[32] – an optimal frame of mind for negotiation. The divine hand seems to be cooperating with Ruth, as it was when she "coincidentally" stopped at Boaz's field for gleaning (2:3). As if to confirm this further, when Boaz finally settles down for the night, he chooses to "lie down at the far end of the grain pile" (3:7),[33] the end away from the watching Ruth.[34] Perhaps this is a secluded spot and will give Ruth the opportunity to take the final and most daring step in the plan which she has thus far discharged in detailed obedience to her mother-in-law, as is obvious when we compare the instructions and the execution.[35]

Ruth waited till the man fell asleep, "approached quietly, uncovered his feet and lay down" (3:7). On one side of them is the grain pile, in all likelihood the grain that is piling up for Boaz to transport to the city market.[36] If all goes as Naomi hopes it will, Ruth will be married to a prosperous man. But Naomi's script has come to an end, and Ruth must lie at Boaz's feet and wait for whatever will happen next.

In the middle of the night, the man woke up "with a shudder" (Heb. 3:8), as is common in a dream. Midnight, in a biblical story, is often a setting for the dramatic. As Hubbard observes, it was at midnight that the Lord slew the Egyptian firstborn (Exod 12:29); that Samson wrenched out the gates of Gaza as he overpowered the Philistine ambush (Judg 16:3); and that, according to Elihu, death stalks its human prey (Job 34:20). In Jesus's parable, the arrival of the bridegroom at midnight caught the ladies-in-waiting unawares and unprepared (Matt 25:1–13).[37]

Here, at midnight, Boaz "shuddered." This is to be expected when sleeping in the open, especially if the feet are exposed and cold.[38] In this awaking, however, there could be another undertone of the divine hand. The same verb "to shudder" (*harad*) is used elsewhere in response to God's presence. One of

---

31. If drinking referred to drinking wine, which is very likely.
32. Bush, *Ruth-Esther*, 161.
33. Younger, *Judges and Ruth*, 460.
34. Block, *Judges, Ruth*, 689.
35. Hubbard, *The Book of Ruth*, 209.
36. Block, *Judges, Ruth*, 689.
37. Hubbard, *The Book of Ruth*, 210.
38. Block, *Judges, Ruth*, 689–690.

these is spectacular, with God descending on Horeb (Exod 19:16, 18); another is personal and eerie, as in Elihu's experience (Job 37:1).[39] Reaching for his blanket, Boaz notices a woman within touching distance. The Hebrew captures the surprise element better than the NIV does: "the man shuddered and turned over and *look*! A woman lies at his feet!" (3:8). We are now looking through the man's eyes, and see the dim form of a woman. It is impossible to tell who she is, but, given the circumstances, she is probably a prostitute. As Block rightly observes, given the spiritual state of Israel at the time of the judges, an average Israelite might easily have welcomed such a night visit.[40] It is impossible for us to guess what Naomi thought would happen at this point: "He will tell you what to do," she had said. It appears that Naomi thought Boaz would recognize Ruth. Boaz, in his liminal state between sleep and waking doesn't have a clue. "Who are you?" he asks, befuddled. This is the second of three times in the book that someone wishes to determine Ruth's identity (2:5; 3:9; and in Heb, 3:16).[41] The first time it was the overseer in Boaz's fields who replied on her behalf – "She is the Moabite" (2:6). Now Ruth has the opportunity to answer for herself.

Ruth is ready with her response. "I am your servant Ruth," she begins respectfully, completely leaving out the ethnic marker – perhaps that is not, primarily, how she sees herself any longer. She chooses, instead, a descriptor that relates her to this man with whom she converses in low tones in the middle of the night: "your servant." Although the NIV uses the word "servant" both in 2:13 and 3:9, the Hebrew differs, using *shifhah* and *amah* respectively. Although both terms mean roughly the same thing – "servant" – and are used synonymously, *shifhah* refers to a woman at the lowest level on the social ladder (compare 1 Sam 26:14),[42] while *amah*, which Ruth now uses for herself, is a more elevated household position. Perhaps Ruth consciously makes a shift in her choice of self-description, to better fit this situation, because she will now make a proposal of marriage to this man.[43]

Not allowing Boaz a chance to ask what business she has with him at such a time and in such a place, Ruth continues without skipping a beat: "Spread

---

39. Davis and Parker, *Who Are You, My Daughter?*, 77.
40. Block, *Judges, Ruth*, 690.
41. Davis and Parker, *Who Are You, My Daughter?*, 79.
42. Bush, *Ruth-Esther*, 124.
43. Davis and Parker, *Who Are You, My Daughter?*, 79. It could be argued from the case of Hagar (Gen 16:1; 21:10, 13) that the two terms may be used interchangeably. See Yair Zakovitch, *Ruth: Introduction and Commentary*, Miqra LeYisra'el: A Bible Commentary for Israel (Jerusalem: Magnes, 1990), 141. Similarly, Sakenfeld, *Ruth*, 58.

the corner of your garment over me, since you are a guardian-redeemer of our family" (3:9). Clearly, this is a well-rehearsed speech, and we need to unpack it. The idiom is literally, "to spread the wing (*kanaf*) over" someone; it describes the act of marriage (Ezek 16:8; compare Deut 22:30; 27:20; Mal 2:16)[44] and could be symbolic of the security a man provides his wife.[45]

Another possibility is that Ruth is idiomatically presenting herself as available for sexual intercourse. Pressler points out that both in the biblical laws and in other ancient West Asian laws intercourse with a woman who does not have family ties constituted marriage.[46] There are two reasons why this cannot be the case. Ruth does have family ties, as Boaz well knows. Also, Ruth makes her proposal of marriage on the legal grounds that Boaz is not merely a "relative," but a "guardian-redeemer" with the responsibility to provide such security. And indeed, Boaz immediately proceeds to address, favorably, the possibility of marriage and to explain the technicalities of the law as it applies in this case.[47] Naomi appears to have sent Ruth to Boaz on a wish and a prayer that, as a kind "relative" (3:2), he might find it in his heart to marry this poor relation who has literally thrown herself at his feet. Ruth reworks the scenario significantly in presenting herself as a legal supplicant claiming what is her family's right by law. What is more, she overturns all social niceties, for here is "a woman proposing to a man, a younger person proposing to an older, a field worker proposing to the field owner, an alien proposing to a native."[48] But the rabbis note the more significant fact here – Ruth's uprightness. Whereas Potiphar's wife caught Joseph by his garments and urged him with the words "Come to bed with me!" (Gen 39:12), Ruth, by contrast, requests, "Spread the corner of your garment over me" (3:9).[49] Boaz asks who she is, and she replies pertly, telling him who *he* is![50]

Ruth has far exceeded Naomi's brief, and by doing so, could secure a future for both the surviving members of Elimelek's family.[51] Unlike the tiger who behaved like a tiger, here is a Moabite who behaved atypical of her ancestry. She resembles neither the incestuous daughters of Lot nor the Moabite women

---

44. Hubbard, *The Book of Ruth*, 212.
45. Bush explains that covering a bride with a robe is still practiced in the Arabic world as a part of the marriage ceremony. Bush, *Ruth-Esther*, 164.
46. Pressler, *Joshua, Judges and Ruth*, 288.
47. Hubbard, *The Book of Ruth*, 212.
48. Block, *Judges, Ruth*, 687.
49. Neusner, *Ruth Rabbah*, LVIII:i.3.C.
50. Francis Landy, "Ruth and the Romance of Realism, or Deconstructing History," *JAAR* 62, no. 2 (1994): 285–317, here, 301.
51. Gow, *The Book of Ruth*, 69.

who sex-trapped Israel into idolatry at Baal-Peor on the borders of Canaan (Num 25).

To have a petition of this nature made unexpectedly, and in the middle of the night, might not guarantee an encouraging response. But this seems to come as a happy surprise to Boaz. "The LORD bless you, my daughter," he exclaims. This is a form of address we have encountered before on the lips of both Naomi and Boaz, showing that here is an older man overwhelmed at a proposal from a considerably younger woman. LaCocque points out that Judaism makes Boaz eighty years old – exaggerated, since he still manages his fields with personal visits and personally oversees the threshing. But, in his capacity as Elimelek's kinsman, he seems more Naomi's generation than Ruth's.[52] Thus, he wonders that she has "not run after the younger men, whether rich or poor" (3:10). In the Hebrew, the term "younger men" as used here can be unpacked to mean "choice young men, men in the prime of their strength and virility."[53] The phrase "whether rich or poor" is a literary device called a merism, and covers the full range of the economic spectrum.[54] We understand from this that Ruth had other options for marriage, and that Boaz wasn't her only way out of her precarious situation of widowhood. Boaz sees her choice of him as an even greater discharge of "kindness" (hesed) than the one she had "showed earlier" – presumably, her loyalty to the family she married into (2:11).[55] The greater kindness is not that she has done him a favor – indeed, Boaz has much to offer Ruth[56] – but that her choice of him has been dictated by family loyalty. What Naomi had in mind by sending Ruth on this errand is hard to say, but Ruth, by her initiative, has enabled Boaz to see not a potential act of seduction but an act of hesed.[57]

This selfless giving up of one's own interests for the interests of the other is displayed at its best in the vicarious death of Jesus, which was applauded and

52. LaCocque, Ruth, 98.
53. Block, Judges, Ruth, 693.
54. Block, 693.
55. Block, 693.
56. Pressler, Joshua, Judges and Ruth, 295.
57. Bush, Ruth-Esther, 170. Stephen L. Cook explores the idea that, within kinship communities, those living have the obligation to demonstrate hesed to the dead – one way being to perpetuate the memory of the departed. He comes to this conclusion by comparing beliefs and practices in certain African communities with those of ancient Israel, including the community in the story of Ruth. "Death, Kinship, and Community: Afterlife and the חסד Ideal in Israel," in The Family in Life and in Death: The Family in Ancient Israel, ed. Patricia Dutcher-Walls (New York: T&T Clark, 2009), 106–121.

honored by God himself (Phil 2:6–11). Paul modeled himself after Jesus (Col 1:24), urging us to act similarly in self-sacrificing love towards one another.

Honorable though Ruth's intentions may be, Boaz still hasn't said if he is open to her proposal. Older people, especially in our eastern cultures, delight in preambles. When Boaz finally gets to his answer, there is no doubt about his willingness. He is perfectly content to take Ruth, and indeed, allays her anxiety with the formula frequent in the OT – "don't be afraid" (3:11).[58] There is no reason why he should be disinclined because "All the people of my town [literally, "all the people at the gate"] know that you are a woman of noble character" (3:11). This resonates with South Asians, for whom social approval often drives the choice of spouse. Ruth's ethnicity, like caste in India, could have been an obstacle.[59] But, as the Hebrew has it, Ruth is being spoken well of by the ones whose view matters the most – the people who gather at the equivalent of the town hall, the gate of the city.[60] It is the same in rural India. The ones who form public opinion are the village elders. So perhaps Boaz refers not simply to the decision-makers at the city gates but to everyone in Bethlehem.[61] Everyone thinks that Ruth is "a woman of noble character" (3:11). The phrase is a perfect match for the description used of Boaz when the narrator first presented him to us: "a man of standing" (2:1). Looking further in the canon, this is the way the ideal wife of Proverbs 31:10–31 is introduced: she is "a wife of noble character" (Prov 31:10) and, like Ruth, "her works bring her praise at the city gate" (Prov 31:31). For this reason, the Hebrew Bible saw logic in placing the book of Ruth after the book of Proverbs, rather than after the book of Judges as in the Christian canon. If Proverbs closes with a description of the wife who best cares for her family, the next book promptly provides a sample of such a woman in the Moabite Ruth.

But just when we think we've reached the fairy-tale ending, there is a twist in the tale. Within the kinship unit in ancient Israel, the relatives of the distressed family took responsibility according to a hierarchy of responsibility.[62] For example, the obligation to redeem an Israelite who had sold himself into slavery (and presumably had no brothers to help him) fell to relatives in the following order: an uncle, an uncle's son, and, thereafter, any blood relative (Lev 25:48–49). Boaz gently fills in a lacuna in Ruth's knowledge of these intricacies.

---

58. Bush, *Ruth-Esther*, 173.
59. Hubbard, *The Book of Ruth*, 215.
60. Block, *Judges, Ruth*, 694.
61. Bush, *Ruth-Esther*, 173.
62. Bush, *Ruth-Esther*, 175.

He is once removed from the closest in the line of guardian-redeemers. We surmise that perhaps this is the reason Boaz has not gone any further than he already has in providing for Ruth and Naomi.[63] The ancient reader knows the ancestral narratives well enough to be familiar with the obstacle motif.[64] For example, Abraham's promised progeny is threatened twice by Sarah being taken from him (Gen 12:15; 20:2); Jacob does not obtain Rachel as wife in his first attempt (Gen 29:23); the route to Joseph's dreams coming to fruition is long and convoluted (Gen 37–45); Tamar achieves motherhood after a double widowhood (Gen 38). Recognizing the obstacle motif as a characteristic of the great stories of old, the discerning reader wonders whether this story is making its way into that category. Will Boaz, like the patriarchs sometimes did (Gen 20:2; 26:9), take a shortcut to get his way?

Boaz's next words give us an indication of what is going on in his mind. "If he wants to do his duty as your guardian-redeemer, good; let him redeem you. But if he is not willing, as surely as the LORD lives I will do it" (3:13). Straightaway, it becomes clear that Boaz will remain true to himself as a "man of standing" (2:1) and will not let self-interest drive his actions. He chooses not to bypass a legal practice that contributes to the health of the community. Rather, he will open up the opportunity for the nearer kinsman to make his choice. Second, the fourfold use of the Hebrew verb "to redeem" indicates how deeply he has taken to heart this young widow's predicament. What is more, the sentence is wrapped in the twice-repeated phrase "in the morning/until morning," indicating that he will act urgently.[65] We are reminded of the contrast in Jesus's parable of the widow who must repeatedly plead her case before a judge who has neither the time nor the inclination for the welfare of someone socially insignificant. Boaz is showing himself true to his name, a pillar of "strength" in upholding the law. Third, what comes through is Boaz's eagerness to redeem Ruth for himself. He swears on it, using an oath commonly used to indicate earnestness of resolve: "as surely as the LORD lives."[66] Here is an example well worth emulating of balancing individual preference with communal responsibility.

At this point, we should stop to consider the legalities relevant to Ruth's case. There are two laws that apply: the law of levirate marriage and the law of redemption.

---

63. Hubbard, *The Book of Ruth*, 217.
64. Nielsen, *Ruth*, 78.
65. Block, *Judges, Ruth*, 695–696.
66. Nielsen, *Ruth*, 78–79.

The prescriptions for levirate marriage are set out in Deuteronomy 25:5–10. If a married man dies childless, the widow should be taken in marriage by the dead man's brother. The first son born from this marriage would "carry on the name of the dead brother so that his name will not be blotted out from Israel" (Deut 25:5–6). This practice achieved two desirable objectives. First, it ensured the security of the widow under the care of a husband. Second, it provided (posthumous) progeny for the deceased so that his name and inheritance were perpetuated. Deuteronomy envisages the enforcement of this practice on "brothers [who] are living together" (Deut 25:5). In the period of the judges, we see that the application of the law has increased in scope. It may be used beyond the immediate family, requiring the nearest relative to discharge the obligation of a "brother" of the deceased.

The law regarding redemption entails a guardian-redeemer. We have collated the various responsibilities of a guardian-redeemer in the previous chapter, when Naomi first mentioned Boaz to be one (see 2:20). The guardian-redeemer obligations are restricted to the interests of a male relative, and protect the socioeconomic fabric of Israel as envisioned in the Mosaic law code – to keep Israel as a fraternal guild of free peasants rather than allow it to devolve into a feudal system of rich lords and poor serfs (Lev 25:23–28, 47–49).[67] The responsibility that would apply in Naomi's case would be the buying back of any property that her husband Elimelek may have sold when he emigrated to Moab. This law does not give provisions for redeeming a vulnerable widow through marriage.

The two institutions of redemption and levirate marriage are never linked elsewhere in the Bible,[68] so we are left puzzled at Ruth's proposal. It is possible that, in the period of the judges, the obligation of the guardian-redeemer could include the remarriage of a widow along with the buying back of family property. In this case, the obligation even covers two separate widows. Elimelek's guardian-redeemer must buy back the land on behalf of his wife Naomi, and he must marry not Naomi but her widowed daughter-in-law Ruth. Perhaps the more plausible scenario is that Naomi (and Ruth) are making an extraordinary request of Boaz to take on levirate responsibilities alongside those of *goel*.[69] Who will execute this duty – the nearer kinsman or Boaz – is to be settled the following day. Meanwhile, Ruth lies down, as does Boaz. Disregarding all possibility of a Moabite husband, Ruth had once promised Naomi that she

67. Davis and Parker, *Who Are You, My Daughter?*, 62.
68. See discussion in Sakenfeld, *Ruth*, 591–560.
69. Linafelt, *Ruth*, 56; Block, *Judges, Ruth*, 696.

would "stay" or "lodge" (*lin*; "pass the night"; 1:16) wherever Naomi lodged. Now a prospective husband advises her to "stay" or "lodge" (*lin*; 3:13) with him.[70] The narrator is signaling to us that Ruth's reward is nigh.

While they are lying down and waiting for the rest of the night to pass, we should respond to the narrator's invitation to read this episode alongside the two other OT stories that were mentioned at the start of this chapter: the story of Lot and his daughters in the aftermath of the overthrow of Sodom (Gen 19) and the story of Judah and his daughter-in-law Tamar (Gen 38).

Lot's daughters are concerned for the perpetuation of their family line (Gen 19:32, 34) and, more immediately, for their own future that appears as bleak as the devastated city they have left behind them. "Our father is old [*zaken*]," the older says to the younger, "and there is no man around here to give us children" (Gen 19:31). In Ruth chapter 1, there is another group of three with the same concern. Though it is Naomi who speaks of taking a husband, it is the widowed state of the two young Moabite women she seeks to redress: "Am I going to have any more sons, who could become your husbands? . . . I am too old [*zaken*] to have another husband" (1:11–12). Both pairs of young women need the security that only a husband (and through him, a son) can guarantee. And, in both cases, the head of the family is too old to negotiate marriages for their wards.

In Lot's case, the wards devise a strategy and deploy it against the head of the family. They "went in" (*bo*) to their father, by "night" (*laila*), and he "was not aware" (*lo yada*) what had taken place because he had been given too much to drink (*shaqah*). In Ruth's case, the head of the family does the plotting. Ruth must "go" (*bo*) to Boaz at "night" (*laila*) without letting herself be known (*al yada*), after he has finished "drinking" (*shathah*). In both cases, a pair of women plan to take advantage of the man at a time when he is vulnerable or, at least, likely to be sympathetic to their mission. While the sisters approach their father Lot (*Lot*), Ruth approaches Boaz "quietly" (by *lot*, meaning "stealth"; 3:7). The sisters lie with (*shakav*) their father in that they have intercourse with him; Ruth lies down (*shakav*) by Boaz after having uncovered his "feet" – a word sometimes used euphemistically for the male parts.

While Ruth chapter 3 is thick with suggestive language, we know that Boaz is no drunken Lot, and that Ruth, despite Naomi's risky script, emerges with her honor intact. The language, then, is the narrator's invitation to contrast the seemingly similar stories. Lot's daughters violate natural law, later codified in

70. See Sakenfeld, *Ruth*, 64.

Israel's legal canon (Lev 18:6–7). Ruth's action is diametrically opposite – she seeks to enforce canon law as it applies to levirate marriage. The results are in keeping with the principle of reward and retribution that runs through the history of Israel as told from Genesis to Chronicles. The goal of the Sodom-raised sisters was to perpetuate lineage: they wished to "preserve our family line [literally, "seed" or "offspring"] through our father" (Gen 19:32). The incest does yield the desired result in the births of Moab and Ammon, but these become the progenitors of what the Lord pronounces to be "cursed" nations. God penalized their hostile treatment of their kindred Israel, when she was at a vulnerable stage in her journey into a nation-state, by listing Ammon and Moab as groups that may never be allowed to enter his sanctuary (Deut 23:3). Ruth's marriage is also "in order to maintain the name of the dead . . . so that his name will not disappear from among his family or from his hometown" (4:10). In reward for the law-honoring route that she chose, she becomes the ancestress of the royal house of David, which built the sanctuary (4:18–22).

Glover insightfully points out that Ruth comes into the story burdened with the baggage of three earlier stories: the Moabites refused bread to Israel in their journey from Egypt to Canaan (Deut 23:3–4); they recruited a sorcerer to curse Israel (Num 22:1–7); and they were sired in incest (Gen 19:30–38). From these stories come the stereotype of the Moabite as ungenerous, idolatrous (Num 25:1–3), and incestuous. Ruth has turned each of these characteristics on its head. She has generously provided an Israelite bread; she has embraced the God of Israel; and she has acquitted herself with honor in a sexually compromising situation.[71]

How does Ruth compare with Tamar? The resonance is strong, even startling. At the level of the plot, here are two non-Israelite women, Ruth a Moabite and Tamar, in all probability, a Canaanite. Both are married to Israelites: Ruth to Elimelek's son and Tamar to Judah's firstborn. In both cases, there is a series of deaths which take the males in the family. Ruth loses husband, brother-in-law, and father-in-law. Tamar loses her husband and the brother-in-law who takes her in levirate marriage (Gen 38:6–10). In both situations, there arises a need for a *levir*; but both women seem somewhat jinxed in their states of childless widowhood. Tamar seems to be the proverbial "husband-eater," so much so that Judah sends her away to preempt losing his last surviving son to her (Gen 38:11). Frymer-Kensky explains that if the practice of this time was similar to the middle Assyrian laws, then a man who did not have a son

---

71. Glover, "Your People, My People," 303–304.

more than ten years of age was expected to take on the function of *levir* himself, or could have set the widow free from his household to find a husband for herself. Judah was probably too superstitious to have anything to do with Tamar, but neither did he allow her freedom, and condemned her instead to lifelong singlehood, with no options for familial security.[72]

The levirate law of Deuteronomy 25:5 narrows down the options for *levir* to only the brothers of the deceased, and may have been a later restriction on practices that were similar to the Hittite laws for levirate marriage, which prescribed a succession of potential spouses for a widow, going from brother of the deceased to father to nephew.[73]

Both women, upon widowhood, elect to remain with their in-laws. While Ruth intentionally makes that choice, Tamar, who is sent away to her father's house (Gen 38:11) till her youngest brother-in-law is old enough to perform the obligation of a *levir*, very deliberately plans to reintegrate herself into the family of her father-in-law Judah. Trickery and stealth are essential to the business of obtaining a *levir*. The setting and the details of the episodes are fascinatingly similar.

Both episodes are set in seasons of yield, one during the harvest season and the other during the sheep-shearing. Matching the quest of the women, these are occasions for celebration of the fertility of land and livestock. Just as Naomi tells Ruth, "Tonight [Boaz] will be winnowing barley on the threshing floor" (3:2), so Tamar is told, "Your father-in-law is on his way to Timnah to shear his sheep" (Gen 38:13). Both know the man's schedule and prepare to invade male space.

Ruth follows her mother-in-law's directions on dressing: "Wash, put on perfume, and get dressed in your best clothes . . . but don't let him know you are there" (3:3). Tamar "took off her widow's clothes, [and] covered herself with a veil to disguise herself" (Gen 38:14). One masks her widowhood and the other, perhaps, ends hers. If the darkness is Ruth's cover, Tamar's is her

---

72. Tikva Frymer-Kensky, "Tamar: Bible," *Jewish Women's Archive*, March 20, 2009, https://jwa.org/encyclopedia/article/tamar–bible, accessed May 15, 2018.

73. See Millar Burrows, "The Ancient Oriental Background of Hebrew Levirate Marriage," *BASOR* 77 (1940): 2–15 for a survey of Assyrian and Hittite laws relevant to Tamar's case, including *niyoga* in the ancient Indian law code of Manu. The Laws of Manu § 62: "When the purpose of the appointment to cohabit with the widow has been attained in accordance with the law, these two [the brother-in-law and the former sister-in-law, who has become his spouse] shall behave toward each other like a father and a daughter-in-law." Ancient West Asian law allowed that a widow could be given in a levirate-type situation to her father-in-law. Given that this episode takes place long before the Law is given to Israel, Tamar does not contravene Leviticus 18:15, which forbids a relationship between a man and his daughter-in-law.

veil. Unseen or unrecognized, each makes their way to a public place where they expect to encounter the potential *levir*: one to a threshing floor and the other to a roadside. One lies down (3:4) and the other sits down (Gen 38:14). If one verb is a euphemism for sexual intercourse, the other is an invitation to the *levir* to make his advances.

Ruth's *levir* turns over in his sleep and, in the moment between waking and sleeping, realizes that there is an unknown woman at his feet. Only prostitutes frequented threshing floors in this season. Tamar's rendezvous is in the full light of day. Her potential *levir* "thought she was a prostitute, for she had covered her face" (Gen 38:15). Both men are unable to identify women they know. Their compromising positions lead the males to mistake them for prostitutes, clearly so in Tamar's case.

Boaz, to his credit, investigates the woman's identity. "Who are you?" he demands (3:8). Judah, to his later embarrassment, acts on his assumption: "Not realizing she was his daughter-in-law, he went over to her by the roadside and said, 'Come now, let me sleep with you'" (Gen 38:16). As the women make their intentions clear, we see that both have the same interest: Ruth requests the enforcement of the levirate law, while Tamar effects it. For this act, both receive high praise for honoring the law, even though circumstances drove them to appeal to that law by unorthodox means. Thus Boaz exclaims, "The LORD bless you, my daughter . . . you are a woman of noble character" (3:10–11). Judah, when the penny finally drops, admits ruefully, even admiringly, "She is more righteous than I, since I wouldn't give her to my son Shelah" (Gen 38:26).

A last detail of the plot is that in both stories there is a gift from the potential *levir*. Boaz gives Ruth six measures of barley, a gift that the recipient, Naomi, well appreciates. Judah gives Tamar a pledge and then sends a gift. The gift puts him at risk of becoming a laughingstock. The pledge does worse – it becomes his public condemnation. Judah shirks his responsibility as *levir* and reaps his just desserts. While trying to trick Tamar out of his life, he is counter-tricked by her and disappears out of his own story, which ends as Tamar's triumph. She gets the justice she pursued in the birth of twin sons. Boaz, on the other hand, embraces his legal duty. His reward is his participation in the line Ruth will perpetuate: "May the LORD make the woman who is coming into your home like Rachel and Leah, who together built up the family of Israel. . . . Through the offspring the LORD gives you by this young woman, may your family be like that of Perez, whom Tamar bore to Judah" (4:11–12).

The Canaanite and the Moabite become matriarchs of Israel. Like Sarah and Rebekah and Rachel, they are childless, till God visits them with sons so significant that the narrator stops to tell us about them (Gen 38:27–30; Ruth 4:13–22). Over the motif of the barren womb is laid the theme of the reversal of primogeniture, where the younger takes precedence over the older.[74] Just as Perez overtakes Zerah in emerging from the womb before his older twin, he eclipses him as the ancestor of David. Ruth's great-grandson David, though the last of eight sons (1 Sam 16), will overtake all his older brothers to establish the royal house of Judah. Even though Tamar and Ruth stand in the tradition of trickster matriarchs Rebekah (Gen 27:5–17) and Rachel (Gen 31:30–35), they emerge as the righteous Gentiles – more righteous than their Israelite foils, Judah and Naomi. Both stories turn on the critical place of the law in the covenantal relationship between Israel and the Lord. These women force the law into operation, and that earns them a place in the history of Israel.

In all this, David's grandfather Obed will have an unlikely parentage. Though he is in the line of his grandfather Elimelek, his grandmother Naomi has no living progeny; his mother is a Moabite, barren for long years; his father is a distant kinsman of Elimelek, old, and perhaps childless, who would have lived and died unremembered.[75] If history does remember these four players, it is because of the choices made on the threshing floor, and to that threshing floor we now return.

It is unlikely that sleep came either to Boaz or to Ruth. Boaz must have been turning over in his mind plans for setting the legalities in motion. Ruth, having no further part or influence on what may happen next, must have been kept awake by the uncertainty of her affairs[76] and also by the necessity of making a discreet exit. So she got up to leave while it was still dark, "before anyone could be recognized" (3:14). Her concern for reputation is common enough in our eastern cultures, and is shared by Boaz, who is anxious that "No one must know that a woman came to the threshing floor" (3:14). It is hard to say whether these are Boaz's thoughts or his spoken words, since Hebrew narrative does not always signal the former.[77] Be that as it may, we can be sure that Boaz's concern is more for Ruth than for himself since the Hebrew uses the definite article – "No one must know that *the* woman came to the threshing floor" (italics added) – in reference to Ruth. In a patriarchal culture, as we Asians know by experience, the sexual freedom of the male

74. Seth and Cain; Ishmael and Isaac; Jacob and Esau; Zerah and Perez; Judah and his older brothers (Reuben, Simeon and Levi); Ephraim and Manasseh.
75. LaCocque, *Ruth*, 101.
76. Block, *Judges, Ruth*, 697.
77. Bush, *Ruth-Esther*, 177.

is at the expense of that of the female. For Boaz, there is yet another reason concealment is important – the legal negotiations of the next morning should not be compromised by the public knowledge that Ruth had met him just the previous night.[78]

But even while all these thoughts are chasing each other in his head, Boaz does not miss the opportunity to demonstrate – yet again! – the "kindness" that we have come to associate with him.[79] He asks Ruth to stretch out her shawl (compare Isa 3:22) as a receptacle for the grain he wishes to gift her.[80] At a pinch, the end of a sari serves much the same purpose in rural India. Boaz probably pours as much grain as the shawl can contain without spilling. This amounts to six measures, though it is hard to say what these measures might have been – whether ephahs or omers or seahs.[81] They were probably handfuls, or scoops with a utensil that came to hand.[82] More important than the exact weight of the gift is its significance to the unfolding plot. Whether Boaz intends it or not, here is a symbol of fertility[83] – for the Hebrew for "seed" (or "grain") and "offspring" is the same word (*zerah*). Though the word itself does not occur in the text, here is a widow who has been childless (perhaps) for a decade (1:4), carrying seed given to her by a man who is likely to become her husband. If she were carrying it in her arms, it might even mimic pregnancy – "Her bulging apron serves as evidence and promise of things to come."[84] But, of course, it is the reader who is running ahead of the story. So do the rabbis, who see the six measures of barley as anticipating six descendants of this union, each having six virtues: David, Hezekiah, Josiah, Hananiah-Mishael-Azariah, Daniel, and the Messiah to come.[85]

At this point, the Hebrew states that "he" (Boaz) left the threshing floor to go into the city. The Syriac and Latin are not so sure it should be Boaz leaving, and replace "he" with "she," making it Ruth who leaves first. It makes good sense to the plot to have Boaz precede Ruth, since that will convey the diligence with which he is attending to the responsibility he has placed upon

---

78. Nielsen, *Ruth*, 79.
79. Nielsen, 79.
80. Block, *Judges, Ruth*, 697.
81. Younger, *Judges and Ruth*, 465.
82. Block, *Judges, Ruth*, 698.
83. Pressler, *Joshua, Judges and Ruth*, 292.
84. Nehama Aschkenasy, "Language as Female Empowerment in Ruth," in *Reading Ruth: Contemporary Women Reclaim a Sacred Story*, ed. Judith A. Kates and Gail Twersky Reimer (New York: Ballantine Books, 1996), 111.
85. Neusner, *Ruth Rabbah*, LXIV:i.4.B–C.

himself.[86] Indeed, it fits well with what Naomi will say when she hears of the night's events: "the man will not rest until the matter is settled today" (3:18).

The "Episode of the Threshing Floor" commenced with Ruth leaving the city and closes with Boaz (or Ruth) returning to it. All that transpired in between these two movements depicts Ruth being as resourceful and as courageous as in the previous chapter.

The plot now edges towards its finish. The audience is confident that Boaz will get Ruth, but must read (or listen) on to see how that will happen.

3:16–18 BACK AT HOME

Ruth returns home as the dawn is breaking, to a mother-in-law who is waiting to hear the outcome of her thoroughly unorthodox scheme. We will be privy to a conversation between these two ladies for one last time.[87]

Naomi's first question is, "How did it go, my daughter?" (3:16). Hubbard imagines "the restless night that Naomi had had: fitful sleep, anxious floor-pacing, frequent prayers, occasional peeks out of the door."[88] Now, taking in the bundle of grain, she infers with relief that things seem to have gone well after all. In Hebrew, her question reads, "Who are you my daughter?" This is perhaps literally asking whether she is still a widow or Boaz's wife-to-be[89] or an idiomatic way of enquiring how the night went for Ruth.[90] Rabbinic reading prefers the literal and sees Naomi asking, "What are you, a free agent or a married woman?"[91] It is probable that Ruth understands the question as a request for news of the night's happenings, for she proceeds to tell Naomi "everything Boaz had done for her" (3:16). Even more literal is Block's reading, the basis being a comparison of the closely parallel syntax between Naomi's question and the question Isaac asks as he attempts to determine his son's identity (Gen 27:18). Block proposes that Naomi, opening her door at a time between darkness and dawn, can see that the person on her doorstep was female, but was not sure it was the returning Ruth.[92]

86. Block, *Judges, Ruth*, 698.
87. Younger, *Judges and Ruth*, 466.
88. Hubbard, *The Book of Ruth*, 223.
89. Pressler, *Joshua, Judges and Ruth*, 292.
90. Given the fluidity of the Hebrew interrogatives, this translation is plausible. See Block, *Judges, Ruth*, 699; Younger, *Judges and Ruth*, 465.
91. Neusner, *Ruth Rabbah*, LXV:i.1.C.
92. Block, *Ruth*, 190–191.

Ruth's recounting of the story is not set out, for this might simply bore the reader. Instead, there is a piece of conversation reported that is news,[93] even to us who were at the threshing floor participating in Ruth's adventures. Boaz's gift of grain was not made in silence. He had said, "Don't go back to your mother-in-law empty-handed" (3:17). Why has the narrator saved this up for later? Here is the self-descriptive adjective that we heard on the lips of Naomi as she entered Bethlehem: "empty" (1:21).[94] We hear it now on the lips of Ruth, whom Naomi had left out of the equation as she summed up her situation. Ruth has doubly filled Naomi's emptiness – just as she has brought Naomi food, she has brought the promise of family, and even grandchildren. The immediate crisis of provision has already been solved; now the deeper crisis of widowhood may find a resolution. Younger insightfully submits that placing these words of Boaz in Ruth's mouth is strategic for the telling of the story.[95] Indeed, these are the last words we hear Ruth speak in the book, and they well vindicate both her value and her virtue.

Since Naomi would have been Ruth's legal guardian as per the societal hierarchy, it is possible that this gift of grain might have been intended as a down payment of Ruth's bride-price. If so, the shawl full of grain that caught Naomi's eyes as she opened the door to Ruth may have prompted the exclamation, "Who are you, my daughter?"[96] Such bride-price, as Block writes, "[W]as often given by the groom at the time of betrothal, not as a purchase price (women were not commodities to be bought and sold) but as a promise to prepare for the wedding in good faith and a pledge for the good behavior of the groom toward the bride in the meantime."[97] Such gifts could be understood as "strengthening the links between the families of those being married."[98] Of course, this explanation would need to hold Boaz's act as tentative and hopeful, given that he was not sure at this point whether the nearer guardian-redeemer would clear the hurdle for Boaz to marry Ruth.

Now it is Naomi's turn to sign off with her last words in the book. "Wait my daughter," she says, or literally, "Sit [tight; *yashav*], my daughter."[99] This forms a neat *inclusio* with her instructions to act at the start of the chapter

---

93. See Younger, *Judges and Ruth*, 465.
94. Younger, 465; Pressler, *Joshua, Judges and Ruth*, 292.
95. Younger, *Judges and Ruth*, 466.
96. Davis and Parker, *Who Are You, My Daughter?*, 87.
97. Block, *Judges, Ruth*, 700.
98. Block, *Ruth*, 192.
99. Block, 701.

(3:2–4)[100] and parallels the closure of the previous chapter which tells how Ruth "sat" (*yashav*) out the harvest season.[101] Now she should wait "until you find out what happens" (3:18), literally, "until you know how the matter falls." Hubbard points out that this turn of phrase carries the idea of casting lots in order to reach a decision.[102] Since lots may fall either way, is this to say that Naomi is uncertain? Block does not think so. Underlying this expression is a confidence that the hidden hand of God, which directs the falling of lots (Prov 16:33), will also direct the happenings of the momentous day that has just begun.[103] If this is so, then Naomi has made quite a turnaround since the time she arrived in Bethlehem, not so long ago, quite persuaded that God had set himself against her to make her life "bitter" with affliction and "misfortune" (1:20–21).

Naomi's confidence extends to Boaz. She is sure that "the man will not rest" till he has pursued the matter to its end "today" (3:18). Across the chapter, her words form a hopeful *inclusio*: her desire to find Ruth "a home" or "rest" (*manuha*; 3:1) has caught in its net an eligible bachelor who she thinks will not "rest" (*manuha*; 3:18) until he does all he can to provide Ruth that rest. Naomi's last words in the book are expressions of optimism.

What is more, as LaCocque insightfully observes, each of the first three chapters has ended with a return. In chapter 1, Naomi and Ruth return just as the barley harvest commences, the first after a long drought. In chapter 2, Ruth returns from her first day in the fields with the assurance of a whole season of gleaning. In this chapter, Ruth returns from her hazardous mission with her hands full of grain and heart full of happy anticipation. The postexilic reader would have taken to heart the message of hope that the narrator of the book holds out.[104] So, along with Ruth, we also "sit tight" to see how the narrator will bring this roller-coaster of a story to the happy landing we know awaits us.

---

100. Pressler, *Joshua, Judges and Ruth*, 292; Block, *Judges, Ruth*, 701.
101. LaCocque, *Ruth*, 106.
102. Hubbard, *The Book of Ruth*, 227.
103. Block, *Judges, Ruth*, 701.
104. LaCocque, *Ruth*, 105.

CHILDLESSNESS: A BIBLICAL PERSPECTIVE FOR HINDU-INFLUENCED INDIAN CHRISTIANITY

Ruth, we have noted, was possibly barren for a decade before she made the journey to Bethlehem and to motherhood. As for Naomi, the neighbors thought her greatest blessing in old age was baby Obed: "Naomi has a son!" they exclaimed in celebration. The loss of her two sons Mahlon and Kilion is compensated in full by her "son" Ruth (4:15) and her "son" Obed (4:17). The belief that God is the agency by which conception happens is not restricted to the book of Ruth, of course. Just as much as he intervenes to reverse Ruth's barrenness (4:13), God plays a part in the stories of other childless women who conceived.

The matriarchs were each well-known for giving birth to a wonder child. Sarah's little boy arrived when she had crossed ninety (Gen 17:17) and changed her cackle of disbelief to the laughter of delight (Gen 18:12; 21:6). Rebekah needed Isaac to pray away her infertility (Gen 25:21). Leah's series of baby boys was made possible because God wished to compensate her for a husband whose attentions were permanently captured by his younger wife (Gen 29:31–35). As for Rachel, her turn came only after long years of envious fretting (Gen 30:22). Then, in the days of the judges, God sends a long-childless couple the gift of the miracle child Samson (Judg 13:2–3). Some time later, Hannah's anguished plea in the tabernacle at Shiloh is answered with pregnancy, and she gratefully recognizes God's doing by naming him Samuel, which sounds like the Hebrew for "heard by God" (1 Sam 1:1–20). When a wealthy woman in Shunem hears her guest, the prophet Elisha, bless her with news of an imminent baby, she is almost afraid to trust it can be so: "Please, man of God, don't mislead your servant!" she exclaims (2 Kgs 4:13–17). In the NT, the aged and childless Zechariah cannot believe his ears at the news of a son and, because of his disbelief, must be struck dumb (Luke 1:11–20).

Across the canon, from Sarah the matriarch to Elizabeth the mother of John the Baptist, the biblical understanding is that conception and childbirth are mediated by God. "Am I in the place of God?" Jacob retorts angrily, when his wife Rachel asks him for children (Gen 30:1–2). If "children are a heritage from the LORD . . . a reward from him" (Ps 127:3), should childlessness be interpreted as punishment? Some may understand the "blessings" (more precisely, "rewards") and curses (more precisely, "penalties") in Deuteronomy to affirm that this is so (28:4,18). Deuteronomy 28, however, should be read in the context of an agrarian economy, one which featured crops and calves and needed large families to manage the fields and livestock. Moreover, the bearing of children was seen as an important blessing within the covenantal relationship with God. Danylak observes that not only did procreation assure the preservation and continuation of one's name through one's descendants, but also guaranteed the enjoyment of provision for sustenance and livelihood from the ancestral properties received as inheritance. Childlessness, however, put an Israelite at risk of losing both his land and the remembrance of his name after death, thereby endangering his dependents' direct access to the collective blessing upon God's covenant people.[1] Thus, if we infer from this text that childlessness was a consequence of disobedience, we should also maintain that all manner of disease were also so (28:21–22), and that those obedient to God would never lose a war (28:25) or have pests and disease attack their crops (28:38–40). We know that this was not the case.

Any of these things can happen for a reason *other than* unfaithfulness to God. Misfortunes happen because this is a fallen world, in which nothing is ideal. In such a world, God allows unfortunate situations in our lives, repurposing the ill to fall in line with his plans both for us and for the kingdom. Why he allows what he allows will become perfectly clear one day, but that day may not be on this side of eternity. As Job well understood, it is God's prerogative both to give and to take away – whether it be possessions or children or health (Job 1:1–2:10) – and we live in the quiet trust that God knows what he is doing. So it is with childlessness. We understand it in the larger context of God's plan for our lives. As we well know, that plan is not the same for all. Sarah had just the one son, Isaac; Rebekah had the twins, Esau and Jacob; Leah had a good half a dozen sons.

All this said, there still remains a corollary to childlessness that rears its ugly head both in biblical Israel and in present-day India. That corollary is the stigma of being barren. So Elizabeth, when she gratefully acknowledges the divine hand in her pregnancy, makes a remark that Indian women might resonate with: "The LORD has done this for me . . . he has . . . taken away my disgrace among the people" (Luke 1:25). In popular Hinduism, anything considered a misfortune is traced back to misdeeds in the past life – bad *karma*. "I don't know what I did in my previous incarnation to deserve *this!*" is a commonly heard lament.

---

1. Barry Danylak, "A Biblical-Theological Perspective on Singleness," Version 2.5, 2006, 5–10, http://www.hantla.com/blog/images/biblical_singleness.pdf. For a detailed discussion, see Barry Danylak, *Redeeming Singleness: How the Storyline of Scripture Affirms the Single Life* (Wheaton, IL: Crossway, 2010), 62–69.

Infertility becomes something to be ashamed of. In a similar context in ancient West Asia, the Lord addresses the issue with a deeply countercultural point of view. Referring to eunuchs – male slaves who were castrated – he says: "And let no eunuch complain, 'I am only a dry tree.' For this is what the LORD says: 'To the eunuchs who keep my Sabbaths, who choose what pleases me and hold fast to my covenant – to them I will give within my temple and its walls a memorial and a name better than sons and daughters; I will give them an everlasting name that will endure forever'" (Isa 56:3–5). Within the framework of the new covenant, the experience of divine blessing is not in being physically born into Israel or in bearing children, but in being spiritually reborn through God and in bearing spiritual children through the proclamation of the gospel of Jesus Christ.[2]

Havilah Dharamraj

---

2. Danylak, "A Biblical-Theological Perspective on Singleness," 10–13. For a detailed discussion see, Danylak, *Redeeming Singleness*, 88–113.

RUTH 4

In a small village there lived a poor Brahmin. Every day, he went around col-
lecting alms. This was usually in kind – some grain here, some fruit there. With
these he cooked himself the daily meals that kept body and soul together. One
day, he was pleasantly surprised by a generous donation of flour. Gleefully, he
took the precious commodity home and carefully poured it into an earthen
pot. This pot he suspended at the foot of his bed, in protection against any
pests that might get to it. Lying down on his bed, he fell into a happy reverie.
He dreamed that a famine had struck the village. The Brahmin made a fortune
by selling his stash of flour. With the profit, he bought a couple of goats. With
careful herding, he was able to multiply his wealth and soon he had built
himself a two-storied palatial house, colored pink, with a garden in front and
an orchard behind, redolent in season with mango and jackfruit. Even the
king heard of his wealth and offered him the princess as his wife. Before long,
the house resounded with the noise of children running hither and thither,
as children do. The Brahmin, annoyed by the racket, picked up a stick and
attempted to restore order and peace. His flailing arms hit something hard,
and he woke with a start – only to see his precious pot sail across the room
and land with a crash, engulfing him in a cloud of flour.

Whether the two widows in Ruth dared to dream, we cannot say. There
are hints of hope, though. Naomi's eyes brighten when she hears that Ruth
has met Boaz – hope is astir! Surely it is hope that drives her to send Ruth
on a midnight mission. And it is hope that moves Ruth's tongue to make the
daring proposal to Boaz in the darkness of a harvest night. There is hope here
in the hearts of these two widows, and maybe the flame sometimes flared into
a tentative dream of what could be. But, unlike the Brahmin, both Naomi
and Ruth not only hoped and dreamed, but also *did*. We shall see, in chapter
4, the outcomes of their efforts.

STRUCTURE

Chapter 4 brings to a satisfying resolution the story of Ruth, Naomi, and Boaz
(4:1–17),[1] neatly tying up loose ends and following up with an epilogue that
spins dizzyingly into the generations that follow Ruth (4:18–22). Like the

---

1. In Hebrew, the opening word of the chapter indicates a temporal disjunction between the
previous chapter and the current chapter, indicating the beginning of a new act in this chapter.

earlier chapters, this one also breaks up into three sections: the action at the
city gate (4:1–12); the events at the home of Ruth and Boaz (4:13–17); and
the epilogue set into the future (4:18–22). The narrator arranges the length of
these sections to match chapter 1: more or less the same footage for the first
two sections and crunching back on the third. With this arrangement, chapters
1 and 4 mirror each other in structure, while chapters 2 and 3 in between
parallel each other with a short-long-short pattern. Added to the intriguing
twists of the plot is the aesthetic balance in the plot's structural distribution.[2]
We shall see that this balance works its way into the details of the plot, setting
up a slew of matching elements between 4:1–12 and 1:7–19a,[3] largely to show
how the problems raised at the start of the story are answered at its conclusion.

4:1–12 AT THE CITY GATE

We are now congregated at the city gate, which, like the threshing floor, is
public space. But the contrasts could not be greater: it is not night but broad
daylight; it is not a private meeting unseen by any but one that requires witnesses;[4] it is no more the world of women but that of men.[5] In verbal continuity
with the previous chapter, the narrative deploys the key word "redeem" but
adds new words around it. Boaz will become the guardian-redeemer who buys
the right to redeem Elimelek's inheritance and marries Ruth. We will shortly
see the expected happy ending.

The details of the legal transaction at the gate are chronologically and
culturally removed even from the original audience of the story (as suggested
by the explanation provided in 4:7). We, the present-day readers, will need all
the help we can get to make sense of the goings-on in the text.

The first verse, as we have noted already, opens with a change of setting
from the previous chapter. While the previous chapter concluded with a private
conversation between Naomi and Ruth at their home, where Naomi assured
Ruth that Boaz "will not rest until the matter is settled today" (3:18), the current act begins with Boaz going up to the city gate to initiate the settlement of
the matter. Although a Hebrew sentence usually starts with the verb and not
the subject, the Hebrew text starts this verse with Boaz's name. Commentators

---

2. Bush, *Ruth-Esther*, 191.
3. The section divisions of chapter 1 suggested by Bush (1:1–6; 1:7–19a; 1:19b–22) are in slight
variance with the section division that we have followed in this commentary (1:1–5; 1:6–18;
1:19–22).
4. LaCocque, *Ruth*, 126.
5. Nielsen, *Ruth*, 82.

observe that this kind of syntax alteration is intended to lay emphasis on the word that begins the sentence.[6] By calling the readers' attention to Boaz, the narrator is pointing out that here is a man who follows up promises with action (3:11).[7]

Town gates in ancient Israel were large complex structures, built with the town's security in mind. Bigger cities might have lookout towers built outside them. On the inside, the gates opened into a passage with a series of rooms laid out on either side, sometimes two stories in height. This was where the city guards kept watch and where they rested between watches. This complex "also served a secondary purpose, as a gathering place for the citizens of the town. This was where the official administrative and judicial business of the community was conducted."[8] This is why we find Boaz at Bethlehem's gate early in the morning. He hopes to catch here all the persons needed for the business he has in mind.

Here is the second divinely coordinated "coincidence" in the book. Just as Ruth "happened" to arrive at Boaz's field to glean just as Boaz came to inspect the harvesting (2:3–4), Boaz takes up his position at the gate "just as the guardian-redeemer he had mentioned came along" (4:1). Here the Hebrew moves into a participial clause to help us see through Boaz's eyes as he suddenly catches sight of the very relative he hopes to meet: "and see! The guardian-redeemer – the one passing by!" Rabbinic Judaism has a comment on the miraculous availability of this man: "Even if he had been at the other end of the world, the Holy One, blessed be He, would have flown him and brought him there, so that that righteous man [Boaz] should not be sitting and in anguish while in session."[9]

Boaz invites this relative, the nearer redeemer, to come and take a seat. From the very start, there are hints that this relative is not going to leave his mark on the narrative. First, we notice that he remains anonymous throughout. Boaz does not refer to the man by his name. The address, as rendered in English, is "my friend" (4:1), but this is only an approximation of the Hebrew Boaz uses – *peloni almoni*. This rhyming phrase is technically termed a *farrago*: "a wordplay in which unrelated and perhaps even meaningless rhyming words

---

6. Bush, *Ruth-Esther*, 196.

7. Holmstedt describes this as "topical-fronting." Robert D. Holmstedt, *Ruth: A Handbook on the Hebrew Text*, Baylor Handbook on the Hebrew Bible (Waco, TX: Baylor University Press, 2010), 180–181.

8. Block, *Judges, Ruth*, 704–705.

9. Neusner, *Ruth Rabbah*, LXVIII:i.1.C.

are combined to produce a new idiom" – English examples would be "hodge-podge," "helter-skelter," "heebie-jeebies," and "hocus-pocus."[10] But the narrator "bleeps out" the man's name. In other places in the OT, the narrator uses the same phrase *peloni almoni* for a place that does not need to be named[11] (1 Sam 21:2, and in 2 Kgs 6:8; compare Dan 8:13). With the use of a *farrago* the narrator reduces the nearer redeemer to a nameless nobody, a "Mr. So-and-so." The rabbis are less generous. They notice that the consonants of *almoni* are the same as for the word "dumb," and they link the two. We shall see, shortly, what inference this leads them to.[12]

Second, the Hebrew construction of the first part of this sentence starts with the name of Boaz and ends with "Mr. So-and-so." In structure, this recalls 2:1, where we were introduced to Boaz. There, the sentence began with Naomi and gradually built up descriptions of Boaz before Boaz's name – the last word in the sentence – is revealed with a flourish. Here, however, the relative merely follows Boaz's instructions: "Come over here . . . and sit down." Boaz is clearly the one in charge. The relative is not merely a passive character but, as we shall see, becomes a foil to Boaz.

Having found the man with whom he should do business, Boaz now "took ten elders of the town" (4:2). "Elders" are men who hold public office involving governance of the city,[13] much like the members of an Indian village *sarpanch* or *panchayat*. These men are necessary for the legal proceedings Boaz has in mind. Judaism nods its head at this: "On the basis of this passage we derive the rule that the blessing of the bridegroom requires a quorum of ten . . . even when a widow marries a widower."[14] Indeed, this quorum of ten, called a *minyan*, is needed not just for a wedding blessing but also for public worship, as in a synagogue.

Unlike the case of the relative who "happened" to be passing by, these elders have to be solicited. Bush rightly observes that "the specific statement that Boaz procured ten of the town's elders is intended to stress the care that [Boaz] took to ensure that a duly constituted legal forum would be present to notarize and legitimate the civil proceeding he wished to set in motion."[15] It is worth noting that Boaz has the social standing to attract their cooperation.

10. Younger, *Joshua and Ruth*, 474.
11. Younger, *Joshua and Ruth*, 474.
12. Neusner, *Ruth Rabbah*, LXVIII:i.3.B.
13. Bush, *Ruth-Esther*, 198.
14. Neusner, *Ruth Rabbah*, LXIX:i.1.B1–C.
15. Bush, *Ruth-Esther*, 199.

Soon the meeting is convened. In rural India, the men might have gathered under the spreading *peepal* or *neem* tree in the village and sat down on the platform built for such meetings. In ancient Bethlehem, the council sits at the gate complex. In both cases, such a meeting would draw a crowd (4:4, 9), for in a small town where everyone knows everyone – and their family stories! – this is a "happening" event that is not to be missed.

We can imagine the gathering settling down – the jostle of latecomers looking for a place to sit, the hurried speculations on the reason for the council, and the noise dying down as all eyes turn to Boaz. Boaz begins by addressing the relative, the nearer guardian-redeemer. He does not begin by talking about Ruth's marriage. Instead, he brings up an issue that we, the readers, are completely unaware of. In fact, not even the assembly there appears to know about it since he opens with a phrase that reads, literally, "Let me uncover your ear" (4:4). That is, Boaz is about to disclose information to the relative that no one else could have told him (compare 2 Sam 7:27).[16]

This news is that Naomi "is selling the piece of land that belonged to our relative Elimelek" (4:3). When it is introduced at this point, we have to scramble a bit to catch up, but that's the narrator's strategy to make us sit up at this further twist in the tale. The story isn't over till it's over!

We need a bit of help to understand the offer Boaz is making to the nearer relative. We start with the legalities of Naomi's transaction.[17] The Israelite law was fashioned to retain land within its tribal jurisdiction (Lev 25:23).[18] Thus, normally, only sons inherited a man's property. In the event that there was no male issue, daughters could inherit (Num 27:7–8), on the condition that they married within their father's clan (Num 36:6) so as to keep the property within the clan. In the absence of any progeny, the property passed first to the man's brothers. If he had none, it passed to his father's brothers, in the absence of whom, it passed to the next nearest male relative (Num 27:9–11).[19]

But the OT has no explicit legislation under which a widow may inherit her deceased husband's property. How, then, is Naomi authorized to sell Elimelek's land? Bush explains that "customary law in OT times was formulated by precedent within local contexts and therefore must have varied with

---

16. Davis and Parker, *Who Are You, My Daughter?*, 99.
17. Millar Burrows has a helpful explanation of the intricacies of the transaction at the gate, tying his explanation to the probable dating of the book. "The Marriage of Boaz and Ruth," *JBL* 59, no. 4 (1940): 445–454.
18. Younger, *Judges and Ruth*, 475.
19. Bush, *Ruth-Esther*, 203.

both location and time."[20] It is possible that in the time of the judges, in which the book is set, a man's widowed daughters could inherit his property provided that if they married, they did so within the clan (compare Prov 15:25).

With Naomi's position as owner of Elimelek's land established, we can understand that she has the authority to sell the land. But that brings us to the next question. Right through chapter 4 there is no monetary exchange. How does a sale happen with no money involved?

In Hebrew, as in English, the verb "to sell" entails a permanent transfer of ownership through a payment made. With respect to farmland, it can also mean a transfer of usufructary rights. Usufruct allows a person to use and enjoy the returns of another person's land for a set period, subject to not causing any damage to the land. Transfer of usufructary rights was common in ancient Israel.[21] Sometimes, it could be done without exchange of money,[22] since the land itself did not change hands. Sometimes, where the seller was in financial need, it could involve money[23] (Jer 32:9).[24] In this case, Naomi has no males in her family to manage a farmland, and she is too old to undertake that task herself. Besides, she needs money for survival. Is she here "selling" usufructary rights to the next nearest male relative of Elimelek for a sum of money?

This may not be the case. There is another word in Boaz's speech that we need to pay attention to – the verb "redeem." Redemption becomes necessary only if there has been an outright sale of land. It is possible that Elimelek had already sold his land before he emigrated. If this is the case, Naomi, as Elimelek's inheritor, may redeem the land if she has the money to buy it back – which she doesn't. That is why she now needs someone to redeem it for her (Lev 25:25–28). On behalf of Naomi, Boaz offers *peloni almoni* the opportunity to perform his responsibility and redeem this sold land by buying it back from the present owner for Naomi (4:4).[25] She will then have land to support her for the rest of her life. What Naomi is "selling" is the right to

---

20. Bush, 204.
21. For a wider discussion, see Martha T. Roth, "The Neo-Babylonian Widow," *JCS* 43/45 (1991–93): 11–26; Richard H. Hiers, "Transfer of Property by Inheritance and Bequest in Biblical Law and Tradition," *Journal of Law and Religion* 10 (1993): 121–155; Pierre Bordreuil and others, "King's Command and Widow's Plea: Two New Hebrew Ostraca of the Biblical Period," *NEA* 61, no. 1 (1998): 2–13, here, 12.
22. Block, *Judges, Ruth*, 709–710.
23. This is clear from the context of the laws governing such sales in Leviticus 25:14–34.
24. Jeremiah 32:6–15 is possibly a clear parallel to the episode in Ruth 4. Hanamel, Jeremiah's cousin, intends to sell off land, and Jeremiah steps in as kinsman-redeemer to pay for and legally procure the land so as to keep it within the family. Currid, *Ruth*, 120.
25. See Younger, *Judges and Ruth*, 475.

redeem Elimelek's land. Boaz now offers right of redemption to *peloni almoni*, advising him that, if he declines, Boaz is the next in line and will take that responsibility upon himself.[26]

The nearer redeemer immediately grabs Boaz's offer with a terse, yet clearly affirmative, answer. Why so? *Peloni almoni* has seen the long-term benefit of the deal. Since there is no male heir in Naomi's household, the attractive possibility is that once the already elderly Naomi dies, the land will become his. Surely Boaz has anticipated that this might happen? What is he going to do now that will reverse the nearer redeemer's decision?

Before the nearer redeemer can walk away with Elimelek's farmland in his pocket – all in the name of philanthropy – Boaz springs a surprise. There is a corollary to the deal. The redemption of land needs to be undertaken along-side marriage to the dead man's widow, "in order to maintain the name of the dead with his property" (4:5). This means ensuring the continuance of "the memory of a person's deeds and achievements, one's reputation and honor, as well as a metonymic expression for one's descendants who give one sort of posthumous existence."[27] In other words, *peloni almoni* is to marry the widow of the deceased Elimelek so that he may sire Elimelek's "son," who will grow up to inherit Elimelek's land and thus perpetuate the line of Elimelek. Boaz's "clause" is well in line with the spirit of the land redemption law in Leviticus 25:24–28, where the logical end of redemption of the land is that "it will be returned in the Jubilee, and they can then go back to their property" (Lev 25:28) – that is, the property reverts to the original owner.

The canon of OT law presents land redemption and levirate marriage as two separate practices. Are these two being combined here in this period of Israelite history when the story is being composed, perhaps well after the period of its setting in the time when the judges ruled? While the matter of the redemption of Elimelek's land follows the canon law, the marriage Boaz proposes does not seem to do so. There are similarities, leading some to propose that this is a case of levirate marriage as in Deuteronomy 25:5–10,[28] while

---

26. Boaz's speech in 4:4 uses the verb "to acquire" once and "to redeem" five times. In all cases, the verb does not have an object. This is odd, especially in the case of the latter verb which commonly occurs with a direct object, so much so that the verb is better rendered "to act-as-redeemer." The focus in Boaz's speech, thus, is on the one who will – or will not – redeem. Similarly, that "to acquire" has no direct object becomes even more intriguing in the next verse where what is to be acquired takes on a complication. Davis and Parker, *Who Are You, My Daughter?*, 97.
27. Block, *Judges, Ruth*, 714.
28. Nielsen, *Ruth*, 85.

others, taking the dissimilarities into account, see it as a levirate-type marriage.[29] The chief concern of the marriage proposed by Boaz is "to maintain the name of the dead with his property." This echoes one of the chief concerns of the levirate law, which is to preserve or to raise the name of the deceased. The difference, however, is that the levirate marriage law is restricted to brothers who are "living together" on the same property (Deut 25:5). Neither Boaz nor *peloni almoni* are Elimelek's brothers, nor do they live on his property. This is why *peloni almoni* will be taken aback by Boaz's inclusion of a widow in the deal. This is also the reason Naomi, since her return to Bethlehem, had not appealed to any male family member to undertake the levirate practice. Rather, knowing that there was no hope in this direction, she had advised her daughters-in-law that their chances of remarriage in Israel were zero (1:9–13).[30] Another difference between this case and that described in Deuteronomy 25:5–10 is that, since the widow of the deceased is too old to marry and have children, Boaz is proposing that the widow who will perpetuate Elimelek's name is Ruth, the wife of Elimelek's deceased son Mahlon.

Taking into consideration these two differences, it seems likely that Boaz is not setting out a legal requirement but a moral obligation.[31] He is proposing that a man who is willing to redeem a dead man's land should go the whole way and redeem it for the perpetuation of the dead man's family. This is why he strategically presented the practice mandated by the letter of the law – redemption of land – first, and then followed that up with an appeal to the spirit of the law.[32] Just as cleverly, he presents Ruth as "the Moabite, the dead man's widow." Is this to present her in the least attractive light to the nearer redeemer and, simultaneously, in the most pitiable plight to the gathered assembly?[33] At any rate, whether or not Boaz was acting out of self-interest in Ruth, his appeal to *peloni almoni* certainly protected the interests of the widow(s) in a world controlled by men.[34]

---

29. Bush, *Ruth-Esther*, 227.
30. Nielsen, *Ruth*, 85.
31. Pressler, *Joshua, Judges and Ruth*, 299.
32. Pressler, 299.
33. Davis and Parker, *Who Are You, My Daughter?*, 101.
34. On the matter of the *kethiv-qere* variants in 4:5 – "I acquire" and "you acquire" respectively – Davis and Parker propose three different readings of the text, all grammatically plausible:
a. And Boaz said, "On the day of your acquiring the field from the hand of Naomi and – *ahem!* – Ruth the Moabite, wife of the dead, *you* acquire, in order to raise up the name of the dead over his ancestral property." Here, Boaz passes on the moral obligation for the care of Ruth to the nearer kinsman.

Peloni almoni has been thrown a googly.[35] He can proceed in any of three different ways. First, there is the option of doing the obvious: accepting Boaz's double-barreled proposal. This would be evidence of his intent to follow both the letter and the spirit of Israelite law.

The second option is to go ahead and redeem Elimelek's land but decline to marry the family's widow. There could be three possible reasons for such a decision: (a) the upkeep of extra family members, in this case Ruth, Naomi, and any children by Ruth in addition to, and perhaps at the expense of, any family he already has – indeed Israelite farmers were not usually wealthy enough to take on a second family;[36] (b) the possibility that any son born to him and Ruth would not only inherit Elimelek's land but might also stake a claim to a portion of his property, thus diminishing the inheritance of any sons he already has;[37] and (c) "the ethnic implication of the transaction" – that is, the prospect that any offspring born to him and Ruth will be a half-Moabite. Indeed, Boaz has used Ruth's full description, referring to her as "Ruth the Moabite" (4:5)[38] – a reminder of who she is. The possibility that an Israelite's estate may fall into the hands of such a one would not be a happy prospect.[39] For these reasons, the nearer relative could decline the widow while opting to redeem the land. This option, however, would show him up as greedy for land and uncaring about his relative's family.

Peloni almoni decides in favor of a third option: drop both offers. While this still would not gain him the respect of the community, it would not be

---

b. And Boaz said, "On the day of your acquiring the field from the hand of Naomi and – *ahem!* – Ruth the Moabite, wife of the dead, *I* acquire, in order to raise up the name of the dead over his ancestral property." Here, Boaz allows the nearer kinsman the gain of Elimelek's property, and takes on the responsibility for Ruth.

c. And Boaz said, "On the day of your acquiring the field from the hand of Naomi *and from* Ruth the Moabite, wife of the dead, you acquire, in order to raise up the name of the dead over his ancestral property." Here, Ruth is presented as legal partner with Naomi in the sale of the property. However, the nearer kinsman has authority over the property only till Ruth raises a son (by some other, unmentioned party) to claim it. Davis and Parker, *Who Are You, My Daughter?*, 100. See further Jeff Hayes, "Intentional Ambiguity in Ruth 4.5: Implications for Interpretation of Ruth," *JSOT* 41, no. 2 (2016): 159–182, for an analysis of whether the reader should see Boaz as a trickster or as a fool.

35. This is a cricketing term, used to describe a way of bowling the ball so that it spins in a way opposite to what the batsman expects.
36. Davis and Parker, *Who Are You, My Daughter?*, 105.
37. See Eryl W. Davies, "Inheritance Rights and the Hebrew Levirate Marriage," *VT* 31, no. 3 (July 1981): 257–268.
38. Bush, *Ruth-Esther*, 238; Block, *Judges, Ruth*, 716–717.
39. Block, *Judges, Ruth*, 716–717.

as damaging to his reputation as wanting the land but not the widow.[40] He makes his position clear, emphasizing it by repetition: "I cannot redeem it . . . I cannot do it" (4:6). This is the exact opposite of what he said earlier, with so much enthusiasm: "I will redeem it" (4:4)![41] If Ruth's foil was Orpah, Boaz's is this nearer kinsman. Like Orpah, *peloni almoni* "chooses the course of expediency and ordinary caution."[42] The reader may have done the same and should not fault him! We should note that the biblical text omits to tell us whether Boaz was married, whether he had a wife still living, and whether he had any sons. If any of these were the case, we appreciate all the more that Boaz chose to complicate his life in a way that the more pragmatic *peloni almoni* is reluctant to do.

The rabbis, however, do not mince words in their disapproval of this man. They consider that he was overcareful about the Deuteronomic injunction that an Israelite should not marry a Moabite: "He was dumb as to the words of the Torah . . . He thought, 'The ancients [Mahlon and Kilion] died only because they took them as wives. Shall I go and take her as a wife? God forbid that I take her for a wife! I am not going to disqualify my seed, I will not disqualify my children'" – by allowing Moabite blood in their veins, that is. What he did not know was that "the law had been innovated" since the days it was first given, and now, the injunction was against a "male Ammonite" or a "male Moabite." Females of these origins were not a problem. "Hence it was now legal to marry Ruth."[43] While all this is very interesting, we understand that the rabbis were only playing with semantics – as they loved to do!

Now we come to a parenthetical explanation. Here is a legal procedure which the narrator has to explain to an audience far removed from the period of the judges in which the story is set. To formalize the agreement between Boaz and *peloni almoni*, one of the two parties took off one of his sandals and handed it to the other. Which party would that be – Boaz or *peloni almoni*? The rabbis thought it might be Boaz – since he is the purchaser, his sandal is given as a pledge.[44] But, though the Hebrew of 4:7–8 does not make it clear, it is likely that it was *peloni almoni* whose sandal was removed.[45] To the narrator's audience, this sandal-removal procedure would have recalled the procedures

40. See, Block, 716.
41. Currid, *Ruth*, 121.
42. Davis and Parker, *Who Are You, My Daughter?*, 105.
43. Neusner, *Ruth Rabbah*, LXVIII:i.3.B1–D.
44. Neusner, LXXV:i.1.A1–F.
45. Block, *Judges, Ruth*, 717; Bush, *Ruth-Esther*, 235–236.

in the levirate law (Deut 25:9–10). There, too, there is removal of a sandal at an assembly of elders at the town gate, but this is not merely to legalize a transaction. There is a widow, whose brother-in-law declines his obligation to marry her and perpetuate his dead brother's line. Such a man is shamed by having his sandal removed. In the future, his family will even have a title to be ashamed of: "The Family of the Unsandaled" (Deut 25:10). In the minds of the narrator's audience, here is a levirate-type case in which *peloni almoni* the Nameless can be given a name; but it will not be a name worth bearing: the Unsandaled.

Having achieved the outcome he hoped for, Boaz now declares his intent with respect to the family of Elimelek, framing his declaration with what was perhaps the legal language of the day: "Today you are witnesses . . . Today you are witnesses!" (4:9–10). These literary brackets contrast with those that the near relative had used – "I cannot . . . I cannot." There could be a whole array of reasons why a relative of Elimelek would decline to marry the Moabite widow Ruth – many of them valid ones. Against such a scenario, we appreciate Boaz for the risks he takes by his act of redemption. We should note that the word "redeemer" occurs a good twenty times in this and the preceding chapter, making it a prominent theme of the book. This is what earns Boaz a place as a type of Christ.[46]

As for Ruth, she is now surrounded by a swarm of Israelite names – dead and living and those still to be born – as if the people she swore to make her people have taken her into their embrace.[47] Boaz formally names all the males in Elimelek's family. It is only now that we learn that Ruth is the wife of Mahlon but, of course, that does not matter now. What matters is that Boaz has now acquired all the property that belongs to the three males named, but the purpose of the acquisition is not self-interest. Rather, Boaz clearly states that his interest is in perpetuating the name and line of his deceased kinsman.[48] Thus, though it is the names of the dead that are rehearsed, their memory is now moved into a future filled with hope.[49]

A quaint detail is the reversal of the names of the sons. They were introduced as "Mahlon and Kilion" (1:2) but are now listed as "Kilion and Mahlon"

---

46. See Lau and Goswell, *Unceasing Kindness*, 136–139, for four levels at which the typology may be discussed.
47. LaCocque, *Ruth*, 131.
48. Younger, *Judges and Ruth*, 479.
49. Davis and Parker, *Who Are You, My Daughter?*, 97.

(4:9), making it impossible to decide who is elder and who is younger.[50] This would have mattered if the sons were still living, since the older would get two-thirds of the inheritance (Deut 21:17). Both are dead, however, and the order of their names ceases to be of importance. Functionally, the names work as a long-range concentric structure across the book: Mahlon and Kilion . . . Kilion and Mahlon. The mirror structure serves as an emphasis, drawing attention to the fact that through Naomi's daring initiative, through Ruth's determination, through Boaz's kindness, and through the Lord's superintendence of events, the dead have been raised. Their names will live on in the generations to come.

It is significant that Boaz's speech foregrounds Ruth by placing her name in the center of a concentric structure, exploiting the legal language which requires her to be identified in full as "the Moabite."[51] That Ruth, from a despised people group, occupies the focal position signals the high honor the narrator intends for her.

A   "Today you are witnesses"

B   Acquisition of the property; Elimelek and his family

X   "Acquired Ruth the Moabite . . . as my wife"

B'   Acquisition of the property and family line; Elimelek and his family

A'   "Today you are witnesses!"[52]

What is more, the next speech, which is the response of the assembly at the gate to Boaz, is also structured so as to give Ruth preeminence.

A   blessing that Ruth will be like Rachel and Leah (13 words)

X   blessing on Boaz: standing and fame (6 words)

A'   blessing that Ruth will be like Tamar (17 words)

Here, the framing elements A and A' overwhelm the usual focus on X by their length and by their invocation of heavyweight names – the matriarchs of Israel and the matriarch of Boaz's tribe, Judah. (Orthodox Jewish parents invoke a similar blessing over their young daughters at the Sabbath prayers: "May

---

50. Bush, *Ruth-Esther*, 238; Nielsen, *Ruth*, 90.

51. Chiasm is a Hebrew literary arrangement where there is a literary center to a piece of writing, with concentrically matching or comparable statements or elements on either side of the center. In every chiasm, the center is where the thrust lies.

52. To Boaz's declaration, "Today you are witnesses!," the response from the assembly is simply "Witnesses!" (4:11a). We must remember that biblical Hebrew does not have a word for "yes." Davis and Parker, *Who Are You, My Daughter?*, 109. Modern Hebrew uses כֵּן ("thus"/"so") for "yes."

God make you like Sarah, Rebecca, Rachel and Leah.")[53] From being "the Moabite," Ruth is escalated to the dizzy heights of matriarchy! Even though Ruth appears to have faded out of the story – indeed, she appears only in a single verse in this closing chapter (4:13) – we find that she is on the lips of all: Boaz, the elders and the townspeople, and, as we shall see in a minute, the women of Bethlehem.

There are a few noteworthy points about the blessings pronounced by the assembly at the gate. First, Ruth is mentioned not by her name but as "the woman[54]/this young woman" (4:11–12). Western scholarship often reads this as a consequence of patriarchy,[55] in which the woman gains identity only by her association with her husband. While there may be some truth in this, it is also true that in some eastern cultures, a person is shown deference by *not* calling them by their given name but by roundabout references: here, "the woman who is coming into [Boaz's] home."

Second, we note the nature of the blessing on Ruth.[56] In eastern cultures, a high value is placed on progeny, especially male offspring – since the family name and inheritance pass down the male line. "May you have a thousand sons!" is the hyperbolic blessing pronounced on Indian brides. The blessing on Ruth invokes Rachel and Leah, to whom the twelve tribes of Israel owe their existence; it also invokes Tamar the Canaanite, without whose initiative the line of Judah would have died out, leaving no possibility for a future royal house of David. The names invoked have local color, since Rachel's tomb is nearby and Tamar is "the ancestress of the tribe and matriarch of the local clan."[57] The rabbis regard the mention of Tamar as effective ammunition against those who, in the period of the monarchy, will cast aspersions on a king with Moabite blood in his veins. "Said David before the Holy One, blessed be He, 'How long will they rage against me' and say, 'Is his family not invalid . . . Is he not descended from Ruth the Moabitess?'" The answer David can cast back at his Judahite challengers is: "So Tamar who married your ancestor Judah – is she not of an invalid family?"[58]

---

53. Davis and Parker, *Who Are You, My Daughter?*, 109.
54. The Hebrew uses the same word both for "woman" and "wife."
55. Pressler, *Joshua, Judges and Ruth*, 302.
56. Similar wedding blessings may be found in Genesis 24:60 (Rebekah) and Tobit 7:1–13 and 10:11–12 (Tobias and Sarah).
57. Moshe J. Bernstein, "Two Multivalent Readings in the Ruth Narrative," *JSOT* 16, no. 50 (1991): 15–26, here, 23.
58. Neusner, *Ruth Rabbah,* LXXXV:i.1.C and F.

Embedded in the stories of these worthy ladies is the intriguing motif of the "bride in the dark." We recall how Leah was passed off as Rachel on her wedding night (Gen 29:14–30). As for Tamar, though Judah propositioned her in broad daylight, her veiled face prevented recognition (Genesis 38). Her father-in-law was certainly "in the dark" when he took her to bed. Ruth, in a way, belongs to this category of "bed tricks."[59] In fact, as we have pointed out at length already, she comes from a nation birthed by an ancestress who tricked her father into impregnating her one night (Gen 19:30–38). Unlike Lot's daughters, however, Ruth has acquitted herself with integrity in the dark of the threshing floor, and she deserves not the accursed progeny issuing from Lot but the honor of building up a nation and a tribe. If the assembly at the gate could look into the future, they would be dumbfounded at the fulfillment their blessing receives, for soon Israel will be governed by kings and Ruth will be the ancestress of the greatest and most enduring of its royal houses, one that will reign for half a millennium.

Third, we note that the blessing of Ruth uses the term "offspring" (4:12, "seed" in KJV). Ruth and Naomi have already experienced God's providence for their immediate need by way of "seed" (or grain) in chapter 2. Now, perhaps, provision will come from God for the long term.[60] Interestingly, Ruth is referred to as a "young woman" twice in the book, and both instances end with reference to grain. First, when Boaz initially notices Ruth, he refers to her as a "young woman" and the episode ends with her going back with the barley grain she gleaned from his field (2:5, 17). And a second time Ruth is referred to as "young woman" in the context of her providing seed (the same word used for either grain or offspring) to Boaz (4:12). We see an ironical reversal in the story. If the hand of the rich farmer Boaz had sustained the poor widow Ruth with "seed," now it will be the previously vulnerable Ruth who provides Boaz "seed" that will make him the ancestor of a famous family.[61]

Fourth, the blessing is that Ruth and Boaz will be like Tamar and Judah. It is because of Ruth's Tamar-like initiative to catalyze levirate marriage that Boaz now has the unprecedented opportunity to become a second "Judah" and, hopefully, go on to sire a great bloodline.

---

59. See Nielsen, *Ruth*, 92, referenced to James Black, "Ruth in the Dark: Folktale, Law and Creative Ambiguity in the Old Testament," *Literature and Theology* 5, no. 1 (1991): 20–35.
60. Pressler, *Joshua, Judges and Ruth*, 301.
61. Deepika Samuel, "Exegesis of Ruth," MDiv Class, SAIACS (Bangalore, 2019).

Do all these emphases on child-bearing mean that, at the end of the book, Ruth is "reduced to . . . nothing more than a uterus"?[62] A South Asian would understand the (perhaps sometimes disproportionate) value placed on a fruitful womb. And surely, in any culture, a progenitrix of kings is worth celebrating!

Enclosed within the benediction on Ruth are words dedicated to Boaz. The two phrases should be taken as synonymously parallel to each other – the region Ephrathah corresponding with the town Bethlehem and "standing" being equivalent to becoming "famous."

| May you have standing | in Ephrathah |
| and be famous | in Bethlehem (4:11) |

Boaz already has standing (2:1) in his community. Here is a wish for a continuance and an increase of it. At this point in the story, Boaz does not know that a story will be written about him, finishing off with a genealogical list headed by him and ending in King David. Boaz only knows that, at his advanced age, he is committing to raise up a name for a dead relative, to raise a child that is not his.

Such sacrifice is embodied in its fullest measure in a future son of Boaz – Jesus. A creedal hymn of the early church describes his action thus:

[He], being in very nature God,
    did not consider equality with God something to be used
        to his own advantage;
rather, he made himself nothing
    by taking the very nature of a servant,
    being made in human likeness.
And being found in appearance as a man,
    he humbled himself
    by becoming obedient to death –
        even death on a cross! (Phil 2:6–8)

If Boaz gave up the last years of his life, Jesus gave up life itself. While Boaz's act of kindness saved two widows, Jesus's act of love saved the whole world. Boaz kept the dead Elimelek's name alive; Jesus wrote the names of us, who were dead in our sins, in the Lamb's Book of Life. If God honored Boaz with a famous name, he made Jesus's name "the name that is above every name, that at the name of Jesus every knee should bow, in heaven and on earth and

62. Linafelt, *Ruth*, 75.

under the earth, and every tongue acknowledge that Jesus Christ is Lord" (Phil 2:9–11). Whenever salvation through Christ's work is described using the analogy of redemption, it is time to tell the story of Boaz the "redeemer." Here was a man who would not "rest until the matter is settled" (3:18), reflecting a God who restlessly worked till the matter of our salvation was settled on the cross.

4:13–17 AT BOAZ'S HOME

The scene shifts to Boaz's home, rushing into a tumble of happy events – marriage, and a baby. We assume that the narrator will comment on how the child now satisfies the patriarchal interests mentioned in the assembly at the gate – how he fills the vacuum in Elimelek's line and furthers the family name. The narrator, however, pulls another narrative trick. Boaz and Ruth disappear after the opening verse (4:13). Upsetting patriarchal convention, the interests of a female get footage.[63] Naomi comes back to take the center stage spot she occupied at the start of the story.[64] This surprising displacement of Ruth and Boaz not only brings closure to the story of the widow who has taken a backseat thus far[65] but, as we shall soon see, reprises the themes of chapter 1.

Boaz, as expected, marries Ruth. The verb in Hebrew is "to take"; Boaz "took" Ruth to be his wife. Beyond the ceremonial sense, the verb may have an extended sense of the locational – that is, in a patriarchal setting, it may also apply to the bride being "taken" in procession to her new home (compare Gen 24:67). A parallel scene in Indian Hindu marriage ceremonies is the ritual of *vidaai* (and its equivalents), in which the bride moves from the "mother's house" to the house of her in-laws, her new family. Traditionally, she is carried by palanquin, escorted by her new husband. This ritual signals that the girl no longer belongs to the parents, an eventuality expected from the moment of her birth, and reinforced by the understanding that a girl child is *paraya dhan* ("someone else's property"). The case with Ruth might have been similar but for this quirk – as she leaves, she takes her family with her. In the next verse, we find Naomi entertaining her visitors in Boaz's home! Of course, this is no great surprise for Indian readers, who understand that parents and parents-in-law expect to spend their old age under the care of their children.

The wedding recalls for us the first hope articulated in the book by Naomi for Ruth: "May the LORD grant that . . . you will find rest in the home of

---

63. Younger, *Judges and Ruth*, 483.
64. Bush, *Ruth-Esther*, 252.
65. Younger, *Judges and Ruth*, 481.

another husband" (1:9). The birth of the son reminds us of Boaz's blessing on Ruth: "May the LORD repay you . . . May you be richly rewarded by the LORD" (2:12).[66] It is in this event of birth that Yahweh makes his second direct appearance in the book.[67] In 1:6 we had heard of him ending the famine, providing his people with a harvest. In 4:13, at the other end of the story, we hear of him miraculously mediating conception to a widow who has probably been barren for a decade (1:4). Whether it is land struck by drought or a womb struck with infertility, Yahweh can reverse the situation (see "Childlessness" on page 103). Even in this, Ruth follows in the line of the long-barren matriarchs, Sarah, Rebekah, and Rachel. The reader anticipates that Ruth's child, too, will contribute to nation-building as did the sons of the mothers of Israel.

As in any household, the baby's birth is reason for the neighbors to visit. It is Naomi who is depicted in joyful conversation with them. It is she who is congratulated on multiple counts. First, the women of Bethlehem remark that Yahweh has "not left [Naomi] without a guardian-redeemer" (4:14). The double-negative emphasizes the reversal that has taken place since the last reported conversation between these two parties. Then, Naomi had lamented her misfortune (1:21); now, her neighbors exclaim at her happy state. Then, Naomi lamented her loss and emptiness (1:20-21); now, Naomi's bosom is filled by the new life (4:16).[68] Then, Naomi asked the women to call (*kara*) her by a name that looks to the past (1:20); now, the same women call (*kara*) her grandson with a name that ensures her future (4:17).[69]

Who is this guardian-redeemer the women speak of? This could be Boaz, who has not only redeemed the land but also – "this day" – fulfilled his obligation as *levir*.[70] More probably, this is the baby boy,[71] born "this day,"[72] to whom Ruth has "given . . . birth." In what way would this baby be a guardian-redeemer? The term's usage thus far has been largely technical but here – as perhaps also in 3:9 – it is used in a general sense[73] for someone who will guarantee Naomi's well-being, who will "renew" and "sustain" his grandmother

66. Nielsen, *Ruth*, 93.
67. Pressler, *Joshua, Judges and Ruth*, 303.
68. Francis Matthew, "Exegesis of Ruth," MDiv Class, SAIACS (Bangalore, 2019).
69. Niss Geo Jose, "Exegesis of Ruth," MDiv Class, SAIACS (Bangalore, 2019).
70. See Bush, *Ruth-Esther*, 254.
71. Bush, *Ruth-Esther*, 253–254; Younger, *Judges and Ruth*, 482; Nielsen, *Ruth*, 93.
72. Block, *Judges, Ruth*, 727.
73. Bush, *Ruth-Esther*, 254.

in her "old age." Whether the redeemer is Boaz or the baby or both, "Yahweh is here blessed as the Source of a steady stream of redeemers!"[74]

The women then exclaim, "May he become famous throughout Israel!" and follow up the blessing with, "He will renew your life and sustain you in your old age" (4:14). Who is the referent here? It could be either Yahweh or the (infant) guardian-redeemer.[75] If this is a pick-up from the previous sentence that opened with "Praise be to the LORD," then the referent is Yahweh. He is to be praised and his name is to be honored in Israel because of his provision for Naomi. If the referent is the baby boy, the hope being expressed is that he will be the mainstay of Naomi's final years. Both referents are possible, and perhaps the ambiguity is intentional as in the similar dual layering in Naomi's blessing of Yahweh/Boaz in 2:20:[76] "The LORD bless him! . . . He has not stopped showing his kindness to the living and the dead."

The expression "renew your life" (literally, "restorer of soul") is the same as in the well-known "Shepherd's Psalm" (Ps 23:3). The image is of one who revives, animates, or refreshes another. This could be, as in the psalm, Yahweh himself; or it may refer to the grandson. Some readers may wonder why Naomi's happiness hogs so much attention. With Ruth finding her security as Boaz's wife and as the baby boy's mother, Naomi remains the weakest and most vulnerable character in the story – a childless widow.[77] This vulnerability can be understood very well in India, where widows are considered a liability and abandoned in places of religious significance (such as Vrindavan) – to remain there in impoverished conditions, with nothing to look forward to but death. By focusing on Naomi's happiness, the narrator shows that Naomi is no longer vulnerable and bitter and that the baby is Naomi and Elimelek's as much as it is Ruth and Boaz's.

Finally, the women turn to praising Ruth. The baby guardian-redeemer has become possible because of Ruth, who "loves" Naomi and "who is better to [Naomi] than seven sons" (4:15). This mention of Ruth's love returns us to her many acts of devotion to Naomi[78] – those performed while still in Moab, that performed in choosing to follow Naomi to Israel, and those performed in Bethlehem. While Israelite canon law prescribes that Israelites should show love to strangers (Lev 19:34), the irony here is that Ruth the "stranger" has

74. Davis and Parker, *Who Are You, My Daughter?*, 113.
75. Bush, *Ruth-Esther*, 255.
76. Pressler, *Joshua, Judges and Ruth*, 304.
77. Pressler, *Joshua*, 306.
78. Younger, *Judges and Ruth*, 482.

shown love to an Israelite.[79] In this, Ruth has proved herself more valuable than "seven sons," seven being the OT number signifying the ideal or the complete.[80] Ruth exceeds the ideal! No other woman in the OT receives such high praise[81] as this immigrant foreigner.

As the curtain falls on this story, in which all ends well, we see Naomi picking up the baby and cuddling him (4:16; literally, "she laid him in her bosom"). The narrator will tell us that the women of Bethlehem continued to exclaim among themselves, "Naomi has a son!" Is all this indicating that Naomi has adopted the baby as her own? (Compare Gen 30:3; 48:12; 50:23.)[82] This need not be the case. In an extended, legal sense, the baby is the offspring of Elimelek and thus can count as a "son" to Naomi. That Obed has two mothers (Ruth and Naomi) neatly mirrors his ancestors who are recalled in this chapter: Perez had two fathers (the *levir* Judah and the deceased husband Er); the people group Israel had two mothers (Rachel and Leah).[83] Obed is in very good company!

Naomi, we are told, "cared for" the little boy (4:16; literally, "she became a nurse to him"). Since this expression follows Naomi's action in raising the infant to her bosom, some have supposed that Naomi become the child's wet nurse. Of course, this is biologically impossible (compare 1:12). Cognates of the word "nurse" are elsewhere used with reference to a male carer of an infant (e.g., Num 11:12) or with reference to "guardians" of children (2 Kgs 10:1, 5; compare Isa 49:23).[84] The obvious, and most reasonable, reading is that the story ends with Naomi enjoying her role of nanny. Naomi had complained that she had been rendered "empty" (1:21) by the loss of the three males in her life. That emptiness has been filled with another three: Boaz, who has taken her into his home; Ruth, who, though female, is better to Naomi than "seven sons"; and the grandson, who will crown her sunset years with delight. The little fellow is called "Obed" (4:16).

The baby's naming is odd. We are told that the women of Bethlehem named him thus. Usually it is the parents, typically the mother, who names a child.[85] Either the women affirm the name given by the parents or they generate a suitable name. Just as in India, where the extended family enthusiastically

---

79. Younger, 482.
80. Bush, *Ruth-Esther*, 264.
81. Gow, *The Book of Ruth*, 85.
82. Gow, 85. Contra Bush, *Ruth-Esther*, 258.
83. LaCocque, *Ruth*, 144.
84. Bush, *Ruth-Esther*, 258.
85. Bush, *Ruth-Esther*, 259.

provides baby name options, it is entirely possible that, in the culture of a small eastern community such as that in Bethlehem, the neighbors settle on a name for the newborn.

The baby's name is odd. It bears no relationship to the comment that immediately precedes it, as is usual elsewhere in the OT[86] (e.g., the naming of the sons of Jacob in Gen 29–30; Tamar's twins in Gen 38:27–30). Neither the meaning nor the sound of the name Obed ("one who serves") matches the exclamation, "Naomi has a son!" It could be argued that the connection lies in the hope that this "son" will be "one who serves Naomi in her old age."[87] And so, in a satisfying reversal, "Naomi passes from bitterness (1:20) to joy, from emptiness (1:21) to fullness, from death (2:20) to life (4:15)."[88] Unlike the Brahmin in the story with which we opened this chapter, Naomi's story concludes with all her wildest dreams coming true – fairy-tale true.

With this, we, the audience, think the story has finally come to a delightful end. Just as we are getting up to leave, the narrator drops his final line. It is a line he has been working towards right from the start[89] but it catches us unawares by its magnitude: "[Obed] was the father of Jesse, the father of David" (4:17). A story about a small farming family suddenly becomes the prehistory of the most famous royal house in Israel's history. The word "Israel," repeated four times, has made a surprise entry into the story in this chapter. If we hadn't noticed the movement from the familial to the royal, from the local to the national,[90] baby Obed now draws our attention to this upward spiraling of the story. Even as he rests in his grandmother's bosom, we are told of baby Obed's future grandson David. This is how Obed will become "famous" throughout Israel.[91] That makes his mother, Ruth the Moabite, the great-grandmother of a king! Now we understand why this book sits between the book of Judges and the books of Samuel. It is the hinge on which the era of the judges swings open into the long and eventful age of monarchic rule.

---

86. Bush, 260–261.
87. Bush, 261.
88. LaCocque, *Ruth*, 117.
89. Bush, *Ruth-Esther*, 265.
90. LaCocque, *Ruth*, 133.
91. Block, *Judges, Ruth*, 732.

4:18–22 THE EPILOGUE

Since the story naturally comes to an end with 4:17, it is possible that the genealogical list is a much later addition.[92] While this may or may not be the case, the fact remains that the list nicely rounds off the book.

First, structure: the genealogy provides the third section of chapter 4, without which the chapter would not mirror the tripartite structure of the three earlier chapters.[93] Second, the genealogy brings us to the final correspondence between the opening and closing chapters. The ten years of barrenness and death in the prologue of the book (1:1–6) are matched in the epilogue (4:18–22) by ten generations of birth and life.[94] Third, the genealogy commences with Judah's son Perez, mentioned in the blessing at the gate (4:12), thus anchoring the story of Ruth firmly back in the beginnings of the royal tribe of Judah.[95] Finally, the story of Ruth reaches completion if it could be shown – through this genealogy – how the blessings upon Ruth and her family did indeed become reality through her famous descendant David.[96]

Of the ten worthies in the genealogical list – Perez; Hezron; Ram; Amminadab; Nahshon; Salmon; Boaz;[97] Obed; Jesse; David – we have already met half. Hebrew genealogies are often constructs rather than actuals.[98] That is, the list-maker often tailored his list to make his point. In this narrative, limiting the list to ten elements may have suited the narrator since, as we have observed, it balances the ten barren years at the start of the story and also places the famous David at number ten. A second hint that the list may be a construct is that Boaz is placed at number seven, a number that signals completeness and fullness. Perhaps the number is also intended to match the remark that Ruth is better to Naomi than "seven sons" (4:15). Here are seven males who pale in comparison to the worth of Ruth![99] All this makes the

92. Nielsen, *Ruth*, 96.
93. Gow, *The Book of Ruth*, 89.
94. Bush, *Ruth-Esther*, 191.
95. "The descendants of Perez are celebrated in two post-exilic texts: 1 Chron 2:4ff and Neh 11:4, 6. The last text refers to them as four hundred sixty-eight men of 'valor' (חיל, as in Ruth) who returned from exile to Jerusalem." LaCocque, *Ruth*, 138 n. 68.
96. Younger, *Judges and Ruth*, 485.
97. It is reasonable to ask why the *levir* Boaz is mentioned as Obed's father, when it should have been the deceased Mahlon. Since the *textus receptus* of Ruth can be dated to David's time at the earliest, we could speculate that, in the decades or centuries prior, Boaz has won himself both popular admiration and a place in the history and genealogy of the house of David. This convention continues into the NT (Matt 1:5; Luke 3:32).
98. See Nielsen, *Ruth*, 971–998.
99. Bush, *Ruth-Esther*, 266.

position seven a significant milestone on the line drawn from the beginnings of the tribe of Judah to its most illustrious son, David. A third indicator that the list is selective is the match with two well-known genealogies, each with ten names: Adam to Noah (Genesis 5) and Shem to Abraham (Genesis 11).[100] By this construct, David is assigned the high honor of the company of Noah and Abraham.

A final remark on the genealogy: by transitioning the reader from the dark and lawless days "when the judges ruled" (1:1) into the age of the monarchy, the book of Ruth gains a status of national proportions.[101] From simply telling of God's providential care of a family of two widows, it tells – we now realize! – of God's care for his people.[102] He provides bread and a baby – and also a king who will forge a federation of tribes into a powerful geopolitical state. But here's the greater surprise: We who live on the other side of the Christ-event can take this trajectory further. "[A] member of a loathed people sets in motion the history of the messianic dynasty"![103] Ruth will have a descendant who will surpass even David (Matt 1:5). Through Jesus, God's provision will extend beyond the boundaries of David's kingdom and flood all of the time and space that humans have ever occupied.

---

100. Davis and Parker, *Who Are You, My Daughter?*, 121.
101. Younger, *Judges and Ruth*, 485.
102. Younger, 485.
103. LaCocque, *Ruth*, 146.

THE BOOK OF RUTH IN INDIAN
TEACHING AND PREACHING

Embedded in the grand and convoluted narrative of the *Mahabharata*, that ancient Indian epic, is the story of Savithri. Savithri was a princess, born to a childless king after long years of dedicated prayer. She was everything he wished for – as beautiful in form and face as in spirit. When she came of age, Savithri chose herself a husband – Satyavan, a prince whose family had lost their kingdom and been exiled to a forest. What was even more undesirable was that this prince was, sadly, fated to die young. Savithri would not be dissuaded by either her father or his advisors. The marriage went ahead. Savithri and Satyavan lived happily for a year in her husband's home, she dedicating herself to the service of Satyavan and his aged parents. Secretly, Savithri kept up a routine of *pujas* (religious rituals) and penances against the dreaded day of Satyavan's death.

On the day appointed, the expected happened. Yama, the terrifying god of the underworld, arrived. Flicking Satyavan's life in his black noose, he turned back towards his dark dominions, only to discover Savithri doggedly following him. The only way to dissuade her from entering the realms forbidden to the living was to bribe her with three wishes. Savithri started seemingly innocently, asking first for restoration of the sight of her blind father-in-law and second for the family to regain its lost kingdom. For the third wish, she made a move Yama had not seen coming: she asked that the kingdom would enjoy the rule of Satyavan and Savithri's sons. The dark lord had to concede defeat. He returned Satyavan's life into his body, and the royal couple went on to live long and well.

The story of Savithri has spilled over from one generation to the next; and, with each telling, it has reinforced the profile of the ideal wife. Married women in India are encouraged to emulate Savithri. Like her, a wife should make her husband's welfare the purpose of each day. She should see that no need of his goes unmet. She should undertake fasts for his well-being. She should consider her life expendable in the endeavor to save him from harm. And it goes without saying that her parents-in-law should take up the rest of her attention.

Indian Christians absorb the Savithri ideal from the culture – inevitably, since they are immersed in it. What implications might this have for the Indian Christian reading of the story of Ruth?

To answer that question, we must consider how the Indian church teaches and preaches the book of Ruth. Once in a while, Boaz is preached as a type of Christ – the one who redeems. More often, however, Ruth gets the attention. She is popular in women's meetings. Here is the ideal daughter-in-law, we are told. The virtue to note is her devotion to her husband's family. She leaves her birth family to cleave to her in-laws, and then proceeds to serve them with such unmitigated dedication that her husband's larger community hears of it and nod their heads in amazed approval. We note especially her dogged devotion to her mother-in-law. She does not take a step out of the home without her mother-in-law's permission; she reports all her doings to her; she obeys her without question; she labors from morning to evening to ensure there is food on the table. Obedience, submission, devotion, service – these are the marks of a good daughter-in-law. In a cross-textual reading of Ruth and a Chinese poem, Yan Lin infers, from Naomi's two dialogues (1:11–13, 20–21) and two instances of silence (1:18; 4:14–16), a disapproval of Ruth, primarily because of her barrenness. In such a reading, Ruth might be seen as loyal even in the face of ill-treatment.[1]

This is not very different from the prescriptions Indians extract from their reading of the story of Savithri, is it! But what we miss is a slew of virtues that we might find culturally unnecessary, or even undesirable. Both Ruth and Savithri are feisty women, women who take challenges head-on. They have courage, the courage to challenge men, either by calling them to account as Ruth does or by insisting on getting their way as Savithri graciously does with her father. Both Ruth and Savithri are enterprising women. Ruth, a foreigner in a community not friendly to her kind, dares to request the foreman of the field for special permission to glean among the sheaves. Savithri thinks nothing of following her antagonist, Death, into the underworld. Both women are ingenious. Ruth improvises on her mother-in-law's instructions to prod Boaz into guardian-redeemer mode. Savithri, by her clear-headed strategizing, outsmarts even a deity! Courage, enterprise, and cleverness are traditionally attributed to males rather than to females. When evident in women, these characteristics could be unsettling or even threatening to the male. Both stories are subversive of culture, each in their own way. It is a pity that we read Savithri selectively, through the spectacles of cultural bias. It is even worse that we transpose our bias-filtered

---

1. Yan Lin, "'Who Is More to You than Seven Sons': A Cross-Textual Reading between the Book of Ruth and a Pair of Peacocks to the Southeast Fly," in *Reading Ruth in Asia*, eds. Jione Havea and Peter H. W. Lau (Atlanta: SBL Press, 2015), 47–55.

reading of Savithri onto Ruth! How much more faithful to the word and corrective of the world it would be if, instead, Ruth could be recognized for all her virtues.[2]

Havilah Dharamraj

---

2. For an article that recognizes and celebrates the gynocentrism of the book of Ruth, as compared to the male orientation – the androcentrism – that is normative in biblical books, see Richard Bauckham, *Is the Bible Male? The Book of Ruth and Biblical Narrative* (Cambridge: Grove Books, 1996), 3–23.

CONCLUSION

Ruth is a book in which ordinary people rise above their ordinariness. LaCocque perceptively develops the theme of "difference" that marks this story.[1] It is easy to see how each of the two principal characters transcends stereotypes. Orpah and Mr. So-and-so are the usual. They live their lives within perimeter fences, their faces firmly turned towards the familiar. It unsettles them to be invited beyond the fences. Orpah puts one hesitant foot into the world beyond it but gratefully seizes the opportunity to retreat. Mr. So-and-so will not even consider moving beyond boundaries. Both live safe lives – perhaps much like we do. But "safe" is not what heroes do. That is why Orpah and Mr. So-and-so are not much more than footnotes in a story of these heroic figures, Ruth and Boaz, who earn their place in the canon's Hall of Fame as the "man of standing" and the "woman of noble character." (In the Hebrew, the epithets are identical: he is an *ish hayil,* while she is an *ishsha hayil.*)

From our very first encounter with Boaz, we see the difference. His wealth doesn't get in the way of his noticing a foreigner in his field. His standing in the Israelite community is not an obstacle for him to champion a Moabite. The fact that he is a landowner does not prevent him from inviting a destitute to a meal with him and passing her food with his own hands. The legal requirement that he should redeem a dead relative's land for the surviving widow prompts him to offer further security to that widow through marriage.

As for Ruth, she is the "deviant *par excellence,*" turning every stereotype and norm on its head.[2] When expected to choose to remain in her country of origin with the people of her kin, she picks the option of a foreign country and an alien people. While the Israelite widow mourns her neediness, the Moabite widow takes advantage of Israelite gleaning laws. Although, like Lot's daughters, her Moabite ancestresses (Gen 19:30–38), Ruth goes out at night with designs on a man, she overturns the reader's expectations by proposing marriage to him. Born to an ethnic group that was forbidden entry into the sanctuary, she becomes the ancestress of a king who will build one.

As with its two chief protagonists, so is the book itself. It transcends Israel's highest authority – the very law of Moses. Where the law provided for the alien and orphan the leftovers of harvests, the characters in this book are happy to allow the gleaner a share in the sheaves and a place at their meals. Where the

---

1. LaCocque, *Ruth*, 151–154.
2. LaCocque, 153.

law stops at redeeming the land, the book approves of the guardian-redeemer whose generosity extends to the land's original owner. At a time when the interpretation of the law results in the divorce of non-Israelite wives, this book stands up and applauds marriage to such a one who has attached herself to Yahweh. While the legal canon profiles the faithful Israelite, this story holds up as a model a Moabite who best fits the law's prescriptions. The law draws a line between the "us" of Israel and the "them" of the nations around. The book of Ruth smudges the line to show us that there can be a little bit of "us" and "them" on both sides of the line – Naomi, who has given up on Yahweh's provision for her, and Ruth, whom Providence leads to two seasons of harvests.

The book of Ruth "rewrites" the law, where Ezra and Nehemiah can only claim to follow it to the letter. Where the latter zealously guard Israelite pedigree, Ruth joyfully absorbs a Moabite into an Israelite genealogy. Ruth expands the law from letter to spirit, just as its ultimate interpreter, Jesus, will do. Jesus raises the bar for observance of the law just as Boaz does.[3] The energy for "difference," for going beyond "what everyone does," comes from *hesed*: the unswerving commitment to the good of another, even at personal cost – amplified and perfected in Jesus.

---

3. Matt 5:27–28.

SELECTED BIBLIOGRAPHY

Alshich, Moshe. *The Book of Ruth: A Harvest of Majesty*. Translated by Ravi Shahar. Jerusalem: Feldheim Publishers, 1992.

Alter, Robert. *The Art of Biblical Narrative*. New York: Basic Books, 1981.

Aschkenasy, Nehama. "Language as Female Empowerment in Ruth." In *Reading Ruth: Contemporary Women Reclaim a Sacred Story*. Edited by Judith A. Kates and Gail Twersky Reimer, 111–124. New York: Ballantine Books, 1996.

Bauckham, Richard. *Is the Bible Male? The Book of Ruth and Biblical Narrative*. Cambridge: Grove Books, 1996.

Bernstein, Moshe J. "Two Multivalent Readings in the Ruth Narrative." *JSOT* 16, no. 50 (1991): 15–26. https://doi.org/10.1177/030908929101605002.

Black, James. "Ruth in the Dark: Folktale, Law and Creative Ambiguity in the Old Testament." *Literature and Theology* 5, no. 1 (1991): 20–36.

Block, Daniel I. *Judges, Ruth*. NAC 6. Nashville: Broadman & Holman, 1999.

———. *Ruth: The King Is Coming*. A Discourse Analysis of the Hebrew Bible, Zondervan Exegetical Commentary on the Old Testament. Grand Rapids, MI: Zondervan, 2015.

Bordreuil, Pierre, et al. "King's Command and Widow's Plea: Two New Hebrew Ostraca of the Biblical Period." *NEA* 61, no. 1 (1998): 2–13. https://doi.org/10.2307/3210672.

Bovell, Carlos. "Symmetry, Ruth and Canon." *JSOT* 28, no. 2 (2003): 175–191. https://doi.org/10.1177/030908920302800203.

Brenner, Athalya. "From Ruth to the 'Global Woman': Social and Legal Aspects." *Int* 64, no. 2 (2010): 162–168.

Burrows, Millar. "The Ancient Oriental Background of Hebrew Levirate Marriage." *BASOR* 77 (1940): 2–15. https://doi.org/10.2307/1355235.

———. "The Marriage of Boaz and Ruth." *JBL* 59, no. 4 (1940): 445–454.

Bush, Frederic. *Ruth-Esther*. WBC 9. Texas: Word Books, 1996.

Campbell, Edward F. *Ruth: A New Translation with Introduction, Notes, and Commentary*. The Anchor Bible Commentary 7. New York: Doubleday, 1975.

Coats, George W. "The King's Loyal Opposition: Obedience and Authority in Exodus 32–34." In *Canon and Authority: Essays in Old Testament Religion and Theology*. Edited by George W. Coats and Burke O. Long, 91–109. Philadelphia: Fortress, 1977.

Cook, Stephen L. "Death, Kinship, and Community: Afterlife and the חסד Ideal in Israel." In *The Family in Life and in Death: The Family in Ancient Israel*. Edited by Patricia Dutcher-Walls, 106–121. New York: T&T Clark, 2009.

Currid, John. *Ruth: From Bitter to Sweet*. Welwyn Commentaries. Darlington, UK: Evangelical Press, 2012.

Danylak, Barry. "A Biblical-Theological Perspective on Singleness." Blog. Hantla. com, 2006. http://www.hantla.com/blog/images/biblical_singleness.pdf.

———. *Redeeming Singleness: How the Storyline of Scripture Affirms the Single Life.* Wheaton, IL: Crossway, 2010.

Davies, Eryl W. "Inheritance Rights and the Hebrew Levirate Marriage." *VT* 31, no. 23 (1981): 257–268.

Davis, Ellen F., and Margaret Adams Parker. *Who Are You, My Daughter? Reading Ruth Through Image and Text.* Louisville: Westminster John Knox, 2003.

Dharamraj, Havilah. *A Prophet like Moses?* Milton Keynes: Paternoster, 2011.

Dillard, Raymond B., and Tremper Longman III. *An Introduction to the Old Testament.* Grand Rapids: Zondervan, 2006.

Frymer-Kensky, Tikva. "Tamar: Bible." *Jewish Women's Archive*, March 20, 2009. https://jwa.org/encyclopedia/article/tamar-bible.

Ginzberg, Louis. *The Legends of the Jews.* Translated by Henrietta Szold and Paul Radin. Vol. 2. HardPress, 2016.

Glover, Neil. "Your People, My People: An Exploration of Ethnicity in Ruth." *JSOT* 33, no. 3 (2009): 293–313.

Gow, Murray D. *The Book of Ruth.* Leicester: Apollos, 1992.

Harm, Harry J. "The Function of Double Entendre in Ruth Three." *JOTT* 7, no. 1 (1995): 19–27.

Hayes, Jeff. "Intentional Ambiguity in Ruth 4.5: Implications for Interpretation of Ruth." *JSOT* 41, no. 2 (2016): 159–182. https://doi.org/10.1177/0309089 215611546.

Hiers, Richard H. "Transfer of Property by Inheritance and Bequest in Biblical Law and Tradition." *Journal of Law and Religion* 10, no. 1 (1993): 121–155. https://doi.org/10.2307/1051171.

Holmstedt, Robert D. *Ruth: A Handbook on the Hebrew Text.* Baylor Handbook on the Hebrew Bible. Waco, TX: Baylor University Press, 2010.

Hubbard, Robert L. *The Book of Ruth.* NICOT. Grand Rapids: Eerdmans, 1988.

Kipling, Rudyard. "The Law of the Jungle." http://www.kiplingsociety.co.uk/ poems_lawofjungle.htm. Accessed May 16, 2019.

LaCocque, André. *Ruth: A Continental Commentary.* Translated by K. C. Hanson. Minneapolis: Augsburg Fortress, 2004.

Landy, Francis. "Ruth and the Romance of Realism, or Deconstructing History." *JAAR* 62, no. 2 (1994): 285–317.

Lau, Peter H. W., and Gregory Goswell. *Unceasing Kindness: A Biblical Theology of Ruth.* New Studies in Biblical Theology. Downers Grove, IL: InterVarsity Press, 2016.

Lin, Yan. "'Who Is More to You than Seven Sons': A Cross-Textual Reading between the Book of Ruth and a Pair of Peacocks to the Southeast Fly." In

Reading Ruth in Asia. Edited by Jione Havea and Peter H. W. Lau, 47–55. Atlanta: SBL Press, 2015.

Linafelt, Tod. *Ruth: Studies in Hebrew Narrative and Poetry.* Berit Olam. Collegeville, MN: Liturgical Press, 1999.

Magonet, Jonathan. "Rabbinic Readings of Ruth." *European Judaism: A Journal for the New Europe* 40, no. 2 (2007): 150–157. https://doi.org/10.3167/ej.2007.400214.

Martin, Michael W. "Betrothal Journey Narratives." *CBQ* 70, no. 3 (2008): 505–523.

Matthews, Victor H. "The Determination of Social Identity in the Story of Ruth." *Biblical Theology Bulletin* 36, no. 2 (2006): 49–54. https://doi.org/10.1177/01461079060360020101.

McKeown, James. "Blessings and Curses." In *Dictionary of the Old Testament: Pentateuch.* Edited by T. Desmond Alexander and David W. Baker, 841–855. Downers Grove, IL: InterVarsity Press, 2003.

Merrill, Eugene H. "The Book of Ruth: Narration and Shared Themes." *BSac* 142:566 (1985): 130–141.

Neusner, Jacob. *Ruth Rabbah: An Analytical Translation.* Atlanta: Scholars Press, 1989.

Nielsen, Kirsten. *Ruth: A Commentary.* OTL. Translated by Edward Broadbridge. Louisville: Westminster John Knox, 1997.

Palin, Megan. "The Mysterious Place Where Thousands of Widows Flock to Live." News.com.au, February 17, 2018.

Pressler, Carolyn. *Joshua, Judges and Ruth.* Westminster Bible Companion. Louisville: Westminster John Knox, 2002.

Pritchard, James B., ed. *Ancient Near Eastern Texts: Relating to the Old Testament.* 3rd ed. with supplement. Princeton: Princeton University Press, 1969.

Roth, Martha T. "The Neo-Babylonian Widow." *JCS* 43/45 (1991–93): 1–26. https://doi.org/10.2307/1359842.

Sakenfeld, Katharine Doob. *Ruth.* IBC. Louisville: Westminster John Knox, 2012.

Schuchat, Raphael B. "The Use of Symbolism and Hidden Messages in the Book of Ruth." *JBQ* 30, no. 2 (2002): 110–117.

Siquans, Agnethe. "Foreignness and Poverty in the Book of Ruth: A Legal Way for a Poor Foreign Woman to Be Integrated into Israel." *JBL* 128, no. 3 (2009): 443–452. https://doi.org/10.2307/25610195.

Sugirtharajah, Sharada. "Traditions of Giving in Hinduism." *Alliance Magazine,* September 2001. https://www.alliancemagazine.org/feature/traditions-of-giving-in-hinduism/.

Trible, Phyllis. *God and the Rhetoric of Sexuality.* Philadelphia: Fortress, 1978.

Wolde, Ellen van. "Intertextuality: Ruth in Dialogue with Tamar." In *A Feminist Companion to Reading the Bible: Approaches, Methods and Strategies.* Edited by Athalya Brenner and Carole Fontaine, 426–451. Sheffield: Sheffield Academic, 1997.

Younger, K. Lawson. *Judges and Ruth*. NIVAC. Grand Rapids: Zondervan, 2002.

Zakovitch, Yair. *Ruth: Introduction and Commentary*. MiqraLeYisra'el: A Bible Commentary for Israel. Jerusalem: Magnes, 1990.

Asia Theological Association
54 Scout Madriñan St. Quezon City 1103, Philippines
Email: ataasia@gmail.com Telefax: (632) 410 0312

OUR MISSION

The Asia Theological Association (ATA) is a body of theological institutions, committed to evangelical faith and scholarship, networking together to serve the Church in equipping the people of God for the mission of the Lord Jesus Christ.

OUR COMMITMENT

The ATA is committed to serving its members in the development of evangelical, biblical theology by strengthening interaction, enhancing scholarship, promoting academic excellence, fostering spiritual and ministerial formation and mobilizing resources to fulfill God's global mission within diverse Asian cultures.

OUR TASK

Affirming our mission and commitment, ATA seeks to:

- **Strengthen** interaction through inter-institutional fellowship and programs, regional and continental activities, faculty and student exchange programs.
- **Enhance** scholarship through consultations, workshops, seminars, publications, and research fellowships.
- **Promote** academic excellence through accreditation standards, faculty and curriculum development.
- **Foster** spiritual and ministerial formation by providing mentor models, encouraging the development of ministerial skills and a Christian ethos.
- **Mobilize** resources through library development, information technology and infra-structural development.

To learn more about ATA, visit www.ataasia.com or facebook.com/AsiaTheologicalAssociation

Langham
PARTNERSHIP

Langham Literature, along with its publishing work, is a ministry of Langham Partnership.

Langham Partnership is a global fellowship working in pursuit of the vision God entrusted to its founder John Stott –

> *to facilitate the growth of the church in maturity and Christ-likeness through raising the standards of biblical preaching and teaching.*

Our vision is to see churches in the majority world equipped for mission and growing to maturity in Christ through the ministry of pastors and leaders who believe, teach and live by the Word of God.

Our mission is to strengthen the ministry of the Word of God through:
• nurturing national movements for biblical preaching
• fostering the creation and distribution of evangelical literature
• enhancing evangelical theological education
especially in countries where churches are under-resourced.

Our ministry

Langham Preaching partners with national leaders to nurture indigenous biblical preaching movements for pastors and lay preachers all around the world. With the support of a team of trainers from many countries, a multi-level programme of seminars provides practical training, and is followed by a programme for training local facilitators. Local preachers' groups and national and regional networks ensure continuity and ongoing development, seeking to build vigorous movements committed to Bible exposition.

Langham Literature provides majority world preachers, scholars and seminary libraries with evangelical books and electronic resources through publishing and distribution, grants and discounts. The programme also fosters the creation of indigenous evangelical books in many languages, through writer's grants, strengthening local evangelical publishing houses, and investment in major regional literature projects, such as one volume Bible commentaries like the *Africa Bible Commentary* and the *South Asia Bible Commentary*.

Langham Scholars provides financial support for evangelical doctoral students from the majority world so that, when they return home, they may train pastors and other Christian leaders with sound, biblical and theological teaching. This programme equips those who equip others. Langham Scholars also works in partnership with majority world seminaries in strengthening evangelical theological education. A growing number of Langham Scholars study in high quality doctoral programmes in the majority world itself. As well as teaching the next generation of pastors, graduated Langham Scholars exercise significant influence through their writing and leadership.

To learn more about Langham Partnership and the work we do visit **langham.org**

www.ingramcontent.com/pod-product-compliance
Lightning Source LLC
Chambersburg PA
CBHW060350090426
42734CB00011B/2095